*The*
# THREEFOLD ORDER
*of the*
# RESURRECTION
*of the*
# RIGHTEOUS

**A Careful Examination of**
**1 CORINTHIANS 15:20-28**

*Containing an additional study on 2 Thess. 2:1-12*
THE RESTRAINING ONE

*Jack W. Langford*

PRESS

# CONTENTS

# INTRODUCTION

The Athenian philosophers and wise men on "Mars' Hill" could endure the apostle Paul's message with a genuine curiosity until he spoke to them of the resurrection of the dead. At that point some in the audience "mocked" (Acts 17:19, 32), as if this was an insult to their intelligence, whereas others more politely indicated they would possibly allow for a later discussion of the subject. Truly, the phenomenon of bodily resurrection from the dead is an unbelievable subject to the lost and unbelieving worldly wise.

### *The Resurrection Hope Promotes Godliness*

Yet, on the other hand, those who have placed their faith and trust in the Lord Jesus Christ for the remission of their sins and have received the comfort of a clean conscience, victory over evil and the resulting consequences of the ravages of sin and debauchery, have a real and confident anticipation of that glorious event. To say it more pointedly, the redeemed sinner believes in his future bodily resurrection because he has already been "*raised* to walk in newness of life" (Rom. 6:4) as to spiritual salvation. Yes, this passage tells us that the believer has already been identified with Jesus Christ in His substitutionary death, burial and resurrection. Paul continued to admonish believers—"Now if we died with Christ, we believe that we shall also *live with Him*" (verse 8).

So it is that Christians can believe in their future bodily resurrections—not only because they have already experienced

God's love and victory in their new spiritual lives— for they also know that God cannot lie! The truth of the future bodily resurrections as expressed in the words Paul wrote to the Philippians (3:10–14) is in the hearts of all believers who are walking in consciousness of God's promises:

> That I may know Him and the power of *His resurrection*, and the fellowship of His sufferings, being conformed to His death, if, by any means I may attain to *the resurrection from the dead. . . .* Brethren, I do not count myself to have apprehended; but one thing I do, forgetting those things which are behind and reaching forward to those things which are ahead, *I press toward the goal for the prize of the UPWARD CALL of God in Christ Jesus.*

If there is anything that the biblical doctrine of the future resurrection should promote, it is godly Christian living. As expressed by the apostle John, "Beloved, now we are children of God; and it has not yet been revealed what we shall be, but this we know that when He is revealed, we shall be like Him, for we shall see Him as He is. And everyone who has this hope in Him *purifies himself*, just as He is pure" (1 John 3:2, 3).

Again, it is stated by Paul in his letter to Titus—"For the grace of God that brings salvation has appeared to all men, teaching us that, denying ungodliness and worldly lusts, we should live soberly, righteously and godly in the present age, looking for the blessed hope and glorious appearing of our great God and Savior Jesus Christ, Who gave Himself for us, that He might redeem us from every lawless deed and purify for Himself His special people, *zealous for good works*" (Titus 2:11–13).

And again, we are exhorted in Hebrews 10:23, 24—"Let us hold fast the confession of our hope without wavering, for He Who promised is faithful. And let us consider one another in order *to stir up love and good works.*"

So it is that honest people, seeking to understand God's promises on this subject, and especially Christians who are looking forward to this great event of their bodily resurrections and wish to know God's timetable or schedule, should all be ready to search the Scriptures daily as to the relevant truths surrounding this subject (Acts 17:11).

## The Truths of Christ are Spiritually Understood

When Paul wrote to the saints at Corinth and clarified for them important truths about the resurrection subject, it was obvious that some of the Corinthian brethren had allowed the Athenian philosophy to evilly affect them. In pride they thought that the discovery of certain realities only came through brilliant research by human wisdom, as if God had chosen to reveal things by means of their own intellectual achievement. The Corinthian brethren were not alone in this presumption.

When the apostle Paul wrote the first epistle to the Corinthian assembly, he gave indication that this letter was also intended beyond them to "all who in every place call on the name of Jesus Christ our Lord" (1 Cor. 1:2). This message is obviously addressed to all believers, even Christians today. In addition, he soon reminded all of a most important principle: namely, that our comprehension of divine revelation depends entirely upon our being submissive to the illumination of the Holy Spirit—1 Corinthians 2:12–16—

*Now we have received, not the spirit of the world, but the Spirit Who is from God, that we might know the things that have been freely given to us by God. These things we also speak, not in words which man's wisdom teaches but which the Holy Spirit teaches, comparing spiritual things with spiritual. But the natural man does not receive the things of the Spirit of God, for they are foolishness to him; nor can he know them, because they are spiritually discerned. But he who is spiritual judges all things, yet he himself is rightly judged by no one. For 'who has known the mind of the Lord that he may instruct Him?' [Isa. 40:13] But we have the mind of Christ.*

Christ had told the apostles just before His death, ". . . when He, the Spirit of truth, has come, He will guide you into all truth; for He will not speak on His own authority, but whatever He hears He will speak; *and He will tell you things to come*" (John 16:13).

Quite often the truths of divine revelation lay dormant in our understanding until such time as God determines to open our consciousness to them. We may have read certain Scriptures many times, but have never really comprehended important aspects of truth latent in them. This is one reason why reading the Bible is so invigorating. Every believer knows that on occasions one can be stirred by the Holy Spirit to become conscious of new gems of truth which have been previously overlooked. The prayer of the humble to the Lord, as expressed by the writer of Psalm 119:18, should be in the heart of each of us—"Open my eyes, that I may see wondrous things from Your Law."

I remember very vividly when I first saw the basic truth which I am going to share with you in this Bible study. I was in Lima, Peru in 1982 endeavoring to help brethren in a local assembly to be in unity on several basic biblical doctrines. One of the doctrines was what has come to be called the pretribulational Rapture of the Church. One morning, as I was making preparation for a meeting later in the evening on that subject, I prayed that God would help me to somehow be able to make the truths about the Rapture of the Church clear and simple to understand by all these brethren. I was drawn to read once again from the passage of 1 Corinthians 15, which is commonly known to be the citadel of revelation on the subject of the resurrection of the righteous. The whole chapter is on different aspects of the subject of the resurrection of God's people from the dead, beginning with Jesus Christ, Himself. As I read slowly that section dealing with the actual sequence of the resurrection of the righteous from the state of death (verses 20–28), I saw what at first seemed to be a very subtle, underlying parallel the apostle Paul was using of the three Pilgrimage Feasts of Israel being the sequential type of the three "orders" of the resurrection of the righteous. When I read it again, even more carefully, it then became very obvious and strikingly beautiful as my eyes were fully opened to spiritually understand the fine and important distinctions which the apostle Paul was inspired to reveal.

### *Basically Explained, here is what I saw—*

Remember, first of all, that in this very context where Paul was explaining the various aspects of the subject of the resurrection of the saints "in Christ," he answered those who doubt the resurrection by specifically likening the resurrection of the body to the familiar wheat field at harvest time. He spoke of how the "seed" or "grain" having been "sown" has now grown up to receive a new and rich "body" of God's own choice. Let us read again 1 Corinthians 15:35–38 (NASB):

> But someone will say, 'How are the dead raised? And with what kind of body do they come?' You fool! That which you sow does not come to life unless it dies; and that which you sow, you do not sow the body which is to be, but bare grain, perhaps of wheat or of something else. But God gives it a body just as He wished, and to each of the seeds a body of its own.

In other words, the believer can now look out on the ripened grain fields about us and, with great anticipation, be reminded that our *resurrection harvest* is coming. In addition, in anticipating the resurrection of the righteous dead, we can look forward to a celebration of having new bodies according to God's perfect design.

Now we also know from the Hebrew Scriptures that God required all Israel to appear before Him three times in the year at what has been designated as Israel's "Three Harvest Feasts." These were most important harvest celebrations. If for some reason all the members of a given family were unable to come, then the head of that family was to appear. Most certainly, all the men of Israel were to be present at the Tabernacle—or later the Temple—to appear before God. This was to take place at the three designated Feasts (Exo. 23:14–17; 34:23 and Deut. 16:16). As stated in the Exodus 23 passage, the three Feasts were: (1) "the Feast of Unleavened Bread" when the special offering of the Wave-sheaf of Firstfruits of the early harvest was made; (2) "the Feast of Harvest of Firstfruits," or "the Feast of Weeks," also most commonly called "Pentecost" in the Greek Scriptures; and last, (3) "the Feast of Ingathering," which was the final ingathering of crops, also called "the Feast of Tabernacles," which was said to be "at the *end* of the year" (Exo. 23:16).

In a similar manner, the apostle Paul taught that the resurrection (or, I might say, the harvest) of the righteous dead to appear before God will be in three stages or "orders." Paul said *"each one in his own order"* (1 Cor. 15:23). These "orders" fit perfectly the parallel of the three designated Feasts. The signal, as it were, of the harvest parallel Paul was inspired to reveal was his use of the term *"Firstfruit* [of the Wave-sheaf Offering]" as a type of the resurrection of Christ, Who was the first *"order"* of the resurrection of the saints (verses 20 and 23). As I noted this and then observed the sequence that followed, the whole simple parallel literally "jumped out" at me. Next Paul made the statement, "afterward, those who are Christ's at His coming" (verse 23). Since Christ was the *"Firstfruit"* sample, it follows that "those who are Christ's" must refer to "the Harvest of *Firstfruits"* which follows. No doubt, this has special significance for the Church of Jesus Christ. And indeed, those members of the body of Christ are specifically said to have "the Firstfruits of the Spirit" in anticipation of "the redemption of our body" (Rom. 8:23). Last, Paul said, "Then comes the *end,* [when] . . . death is destroyed [or abolished]" (verses 24–26). Sequentially, this would have reference to the resurrection of the Old Testament and Tribulation saints, which would be represented by the "Feast of [final] Ingathering at the *end* of the year" (Exo. 23:16).

There it was, an outline of the whole plan of God regarding the resurrections of the righteous, plain and simple, following the harvest sequence! How many times in the past other brethren and I had sought for a clear explanation of this passage of Scripture which seemed to elude us! I can assure you, this has also been true of many theologians and Bible teachers, especially in these very last days.

At that time in Peru I studied the passage more carefully. There it remained, clear and sensible. That evening I immediately shared it with the brethren there in Peru in a very simplified form as a basis for studying the subject of the Rapture. It helped them greatly.

Now I want to share it with you in a much more thorough and careful, step by step procedure because, of course, it must be clearly and consistently proven from a complete and thorough examination of all relevant Scriptures. In addition, it must be able to stand any test of criticism. And this testing is what Paul exhorted brethren to do—"But examine everything carefully; hold fast to that which is good" (1 Thess. 5:21, NASB).

## A Most Important Subject

We know that the basic issue of Christ's bodily resurrection is absolutely fundamental to the Christian faith—"And if Christ is not risen, your faith is futile; you are still in your sins!" (1 Cor. 15:17). In addition, all the aspects of the resurrection subject with which Paul dealt in this chapter of 1 Corinthians are vitally relative to our lives and hope.

Furthermore, this is a very important subject, the outcome of which gives clear and positive solutions to some basic problems causing confusion in the minds of many Christians. These areas of confusion involve, on the one hand, the distinction between the resurrection of the Old Testament saints and the Rapture of the Church and, on the other hand, the timing of the resurrection and Rapture of the Church. The proper interpretation of this passage of Scripture is crucial to our realizing the sequences in the resurrection of the righteous dead in relation to the end time events.

For us today, with world events pressing forward in prophetic alignment as never before, a clear understanding of this passage of Scripture is an absolute prerequisite for our comprehension of the uniqueness of the Rapture of the Church—separate and distinct from the resurrection of the Old Testament and Tribulation saints which will be at the end of the time of the Great Tribulation. If there are, indeed, as I am intending to prove in this study, three "orders" to the resurrection of the righteous, then this fact alone would conclusively prove and demonstrate the uniqueness of the Rapture of the Church before the time of the Great Tribulation. Therefore, if there ever was a clear demonstration and positive proof of the distinctive pretribulational Rapture of the Church, it is most certainly found here in 1 Corinthians 15.

I believe we shall find that 1 Corinthians 15:20–28 stands as a divinely inspired *blueprint* for the "orders" and sequencing of the theme of the resurrection of the righteous in dispensational time. The Holy Spirit, as the Divine Architect, has drawn up God's plans on this vital subject, and has presented before us these plans through His servant, Paul, here in 1 Corinthians 15 in order that God's people might see, understand and be comforted in their perception of what is before us. Once we carefully look at and understand these *blueprints,* we will not only know of our distinctive departure from this earth but, by comparing other related Scriptures as well, we can know more surely the *timing of our departure* relative to prophesied end time events. Once we have traversed through this passage in a very careful manner, I believe you will agree with me and rejoice in the truth as well. Jesus Christ has not intended that we remain ignorant about this subject. It seems that we have been uninformed for a long time about the vital importance of this passage in 1 Corinthians 15.

I do not make a claim to originality in understanding this subject. Others have also had glimpses of this basic truth—I will list those of whom I know in the Appendix. However, it is amazing to me that so few, if any, have ever expounded in depth upon this truth from this passage of Scripture. If someone has, I have never read it. In this regard, what you are going to be reading may very well be a whole new field of realization on this wonderful and vitally important theme.

In order to understand this in a positive way, and to allow criticism to be focused upon it, I will need to go through 1 Corinthians 15:20-28 in a very slow and careful manner, verse by verse, step by step and subject by subject. I hope you will be prepared for such a study. I am sure that in the end you will be rewarded for your patience and perseverance.

Throughout this manuscript I have chosen to emphasize the primary words describing the special Feasts and Offerings in Israel's liturgical calendar by capitalizing them. In addition, I am capitalizing the words Church and Rapture simply to denote the absolute uniqueness of God's called-out congregation of saints in this Age of Grace, and the absolute uniqueness of their departure from this earth.

In preparation for this investigation there are several things we need to understand—

*Chapter One*

# PRELIMINARY INFORMATION

## *Two Kinds of Resurrection*

F*irst of all*, it is important to remember that the Scriptures reveal two entirely different kinds of resurrection of the dead. The Bible clearly reveals that everyone will be resurrected from the dead, both the saved and the unsaved. The resurrection of these two different categories of people will be for vastly different reasons and will take place at different times. They will not happen simultaneously. We must understand this so that we do not mingle the resurrection of the unsaved with that of the saved—or with any of the "orders" of the resurrection of the saved.

The first passage illustrating the two distinct kinds of resurrection which we will read is John 5:28 and 29 where Christ said, "Do not marvel at this; for the hour is coming in which all who are in the graves will hear His voice and come forth—those who have done good, *to the resurrection of life,* and those who have done evil, *to the resurrection of condemnation."* The prophet Daniel also spoke of this in the following words, "And many of those who sleep in the dust of the earth shall awake, *some to everlasting life, some to shame and everlasting contempt"* (Dan. 12:2). The apostle Paul designated these two events as "a resurrection of the dead, *both the just and the unjust"* (Acts 24:15). In the last book of the Bible, the apostle

John referred to the resurrection of the saints martyred during the Great Tribulation as being a part of *"the first resurrection"* (Rev. 20:4–6). In contrast, John also designated the resurrection of the unjust as *"the second death"* (Rev. 20:6 and 14). And lest anyone thinks that these two resurrections happen at the same time, John made an important clarification that the resurrections of these two categories of people, the just and the unjust, are separated by the "thousand year" reign of the Messiah (Rev. 20:5 and 13–15). As to the specific statement separating these two events, the resurrection of the unrighteous will not take place *"until the thousand years were finished"* (Rev. 20:5). This resurrection of the unsaved is directly associated with *"the second death"* as specified in Revelation 20:6 and 14. So it is, the righteous will have no part in *"the second death,"* and the unrighteous will have no part in *"the first resurrection."*

| Kinds— | Resurrection of Saved | Resurrection of Unsaved |
|---|---|---|
| John 5:28, 29 | "Resurrection of Life" | "Resurrection of Condemnation" |
| Dan. 12:2 | "To Everlasting Life" | "To . . . Everlasting Contempt" |
| Acts 24:15 | "The Just" | "The Unjust" |
| Rev. 20:4–6 | "The First Resurrection" | "The Second Death" |

It is highly important that these two distinct categories of resurrection never be mingled together. The righteous will get *"glorified bodies,"* whereas the unrighteous are not said to get such bodies; they will be resurrected in their mortal bodies. The righteous will be in a place and position of bliss and glory, whereas the wicked will be in *"shame and everlasting contempt."* *"Death,"* as the enemy of the righteous, will have been *"destroyed."* Death was "destroyed" **spiritually** at Christ's first coming when "He tasted death for every man" and brought "life and immortality to light through the gospel" (Heb. 2:9 and 2 Tim. 1:10). He will have "abolished death" **physically** and in completion at His second coming with the final "order" of the resurrection of the righteous. This is not true for the unrighteous. *"Death"* is not destroyed for them. As was already stated, their resurrection is associated with *"the second death."* "Death," as a condition of continued existence in *separation* from God, will be the fate of the lost. It will be most important to remember that Paul did not speak of the resurrection of the lost in 1 Corinthians 15. The resurrection of the unjust will take place at the end of the thousand year reign of Christ just before the creation of the new heavens and new earth.

It would also be appropriate at this time to clarify what it means to be one of the "righteous or just" and also what it means to "have done good" as Christ spoke in John 5:29. The "just" are only righteous because of their faith in the Lord Jesus Christ (Rom. 3:22 and 4:5) as their sin-bearer and substitute, Who paid the penalty for their sins in His sacrificial death. Christ died for the sins of all mankind. However, only those who place their faith in Christ are said to be "justified" and "made righteous." All our sins were "imputed" to Jesus Christ when He died the sinners' death. On the cross *"He* [God the Father] *made Him* [Christ] *Who knew no sin to be sin for us, that we might be made the righteousness of God in Him"* (2 Cor. 5:21). All Christ's perfect "righteousness" was imputed to the believer in the resurrection of Christ from the dead (Rom. 5:17 and 6:7–11) so that now, in the sight of God, the believer stands in the righteousness of Jesus Christ. Likewise, as to "doing good works," let it be known first of all that *"this is the work of God, that you believe in Him Whom He has sent"* (John 6:29). This is the only "work" that the helpless sinner can do in order to be saved (Acts 16:30, 31). The one who has placed his faith in Jesus Christ is then *"created in Christ Jesus for good works, which God prepared beforehand that we should walk in them"* (Eph. 2:10). So, to be qualified for the resurrection of "the just," and to be one who has "done good," is first of all to have placed your faith and trust in Jesus Christ as the gracious Savior and Lord of your life.

### *Three "Orders" of the Resurrection of the Righteous*

*Second*, it is also very important to recognize that the resurrection of the righteous will not take place all at once, at the same time, or in the same event. As I stated before, in 1 Corinthians 15 the apostle Paul revealed to us that the resurrection of the righteous dead will be in different stages or "order[s]" (1 Cor. 15:23). Some interpreters think there are only two "orders" in this resurrection, whereas others recognize that there are three "orders." Let me assure you, we will study this very carefully in the next chapter. The last "order" being at "the end" (1 Cor. 15: 24) is also spoken of in Revelation 20:4. We shall find that this last "order" takes place at "the end" time event of the second coming of Jesus Christ to rule and reign on earth. This happens at the very beginning of the thousand year reign of Christ. Many interpreters confuse the resurrection of the *"unjust"* with the last *"order"* of the resurrection of the righteous.

Furthermore, the fact that there are different "orders" to the resurrection of the righteous should be very helpful in distinguishing in our minds the different *groups* designated for each "order" and the different *times* when God will resurrect the righteous dead. The three Pilgrimage Feasts of Israel, which centered around the harvest theme, were held on entirely different dates of the harvest calendar. And likewise, so are the resurrection harvests of the righteous. If all in the families could not come to Jerusalem for these Feasts, then the heads of households were required to attend as representatives of their households on these three occasions. There was not ONE super-large harvest Feast; nor is there one super-large resurrection harvest of the righteous. Rather, there were three distinct Feasts for Israel in the counsels of God. Each was on a different date of the year. In a similar way, since we will find that there are three occasions in which God will resurrect the righteous, we should not try to blend them together, or equate any of these "orders" with the resurrection of the wicked. Each group or "order" of the righteous will be raised from the dead at its own time, with its own *company* of saints and with its own *distinction* from the others. This fact will settle a whole lot of confusion on the subject.

### *An Outline of 1 Corinthians 15 in six (6) sections; with Emphasis on Verses 20–28,*

1. A basic element in the Gospel proclamation is the resurrection of Jesus Christ from the dead (verses 1–11);

2. The futility of our preaching the truths about Christ if Christ is not raised from the dead (verses 12–19);

**3. The sequence of the resurrection of the righteous in three "companies" or "orders" (verses 20–28);**

4. The proof of the resurrection from the dead by the believers suffering willingly (verses 29–34);

5. The types of resurrection bodies and the distinction between earthly and heavenly bodies (verses 35–49);

6. The revelation of the mystery clearly spelled out—the Rapture of the Church saints of this age (verses 50–58).

In focusing our attention on verses 20–28 (section 3), I will print them in a way which will make it easier to comprehend them without doing any damage to the text. I will place certain words and the quotes from the Hebrew Scriptures **in bold**. It is important to be aware of exactly what is being quoted. I will also indent certain portions in order to visually perceive their position in relationship to the whole of what is being said. In other words, some statements are subservient to and qualifiers of other statements. Certain words I will *italicize* and <u>underline</u> for further emphasis. When we thus separate the passage into these parts or sections, I believe we might be better able to grasp the understanding (or perspective) of the last section especially. The last parts of this section, verse 24 through verse 28, are all *qualifiers* concerning the third "order" of the resurrection of the righteous. In my translation of these verses, I am going to be checking with the New American Standard Bible, several of the Greek-English Interlinears and the New King James Version. So this will be slightly different from any single translation. This is being done for no other reason than for accurateness.

### *Formatting the Text of 1 Corinthians 15:20–28*

Verse—

20. But now Christ has been raised from the dead, [and has become] the **'Firstfruit'** of those who have fallen asleep.

21. For since through a man came death, also through a Man came the resurrection of the dead.

22. For as **in Adam** all die, even so **in Christ** shall all be made alive.

23. But each in his own *order* [company or rank]:
    [1] *Christ* the *'Firstfruit,'*
    [2] *afterward, those who are Christ's at His coming,*

24. [3] *then* **the end,**
    when He delivers up the Kingdom to God even the Father,
    when He abolishes all rule and all authority and power.

25. For He must reign **'till He puts all enemies under His feet'** [Psalm 110:1].

26. *The last enemy to be abolished* [or destroyed] *is death.* For **'He has put all things in subjection under His feet'** [Psalm 8:6]. But when He says that **'All things are put in subjection,'** it is evident that He Who put all things in subjection to Him is excepted. But when all things are subjected to Him, then also will the Son, Himself, be subjected to the One having subjected all things to Him, in order that God may be All in All.

I am sure, as we go through this study, that you will want to return again and again to these Scriptures to align yourself with the facts which the apostle Paul is giving. We are going to start with verse 20 and go through each of the verses very slowly and carefully because each and every statement is very important.

## Chapter Two

# PREPARATORY VERSES

### *"FIRSTFRUIT"* (Verse 20)

T he word which signals our interest at the start of this section
of Scripture is the word *"Firstfruit"* (or firstfruits). In Christ's
resurrection from the dead, He is said to be the "Firstfruit" of those
saints who have fallen asleep in death (verse 20). This word stands,
therefore, as an insignia of the discussion which is to follow. Paul
will repeat it again in verse 23—"Christ the Firstfruit." Thus it is
waved like a banner at the beginning of this very important section.
To carefully understand it and to note its importance, one must go
back to what has been called the three "Pilgrimage Feasts" of Israel—
where the Israelites were to appear before God at the designated
place. These are also looked upon as the "Harvest Feasts" of Israel.

First, there was the Feast of Unleavened Bread which is
sometimes also called Passover, since the Passover meal was
eaten on the evening beginning this Feast of seven days of eating
unleavened bread. It was at a *designated time* during this Feast that
the special offering of the "Firstfruits" was to be made (see Lev.
23:10, 11). Many Christian expositors today have erroneously made
reference to this offering as if it were a separate "Feast." It is not
so understood in Jewish reckoning and celebrations. The actual
Hebrew word for feast is *chag* or *haggim* (plural), meaning to move

in a circle, dance, celebrate—hence, a feast or festival. This word is never used of this special offering. It was simply a special offering to be made at an "appointed time" (Hebrew, *mowed* or *mo'adim*, plural) during the Feast of Unleavened Bread. The offering was in the form of a "sheaf" or bundle of the first or early sample of grain to be harvested. Sometimes this "Sheaf" was called by its Hebrew name, *"Omer,"* which has reference to the particular measure of grain in the sheaf (see Exo.16:36). This "Sheaf of Firstfruits" was to be *"waved"* up in the air (Lev. 23:11) on a Sunday morning which occurred during that Feast. I will have more to say about the timing of this offering later. I say again, this offering was not a separate Feast, in and of itself, as is often erroneously stated by many Bible teachers. It was simply a very special offering which was made at a particular time during the Feast of Unleavened Bread.

This first Feast of Unleavened Bread was actually not a harvest Feast, whereas the last two Feasts were specifically centered on the two times of harvesting in Israel. However, this first Feast took upon itself a harvest theme by this particular offering of the freshly cut early grain of the *"Sheaf of Firstfruits"* which was to be waved up in the air. This special offering was intended as a sample, token or guarantee of the blessed full harvest which was to come later. The full spring harvest would be celebrated at another Feast exactly fifty days later after this specific offering was made. We will come back to this special offering of "Firstfruit" shortly.

The second Feast was called by several different names. It is sometimes called "the Feast of Firstfruits" because it involved the spring harvest of firstfruits (Exo.23:16; 34:22; Lev. 23:17 and Num. 28:26). This spring harvest Feast is most often called today "the Feast of Weeks" (Heb., *Shavuot,* Exo. 34:22; Num. 28:26; and Deut. 16:10) because they would count off seven weeks from the offering of the "Wave-sheaf" during the Feast of Unleavened Bread. Then after the seven *weeks* had been counted (49 days), on the early morning of the next or *fiftieth* day they would have the celebration, as the Jews would say, of *Shavuot* (Weeks). A third designation for this Feast is the Greek word *Pentecost* which means "fiftieth." This is what it is commonly called in the Gentile world and this is the designation which is used in the book of Acts chapter two (see also

Acts 20:16 and 1 Cor. 16:8). The main characterization of this Feast was the offering of a portion of the harvested grain in the form of *"two loaves of bread waved up before the Lord"* exactly as they had done fifty days earlier with the "Wave-sheaf" of early grain. And here we see the vital interrelationship between these two offerings. We will also come back to this later.

The third and final Pilgrimage Feast of the year also had several different designations. It is called "the Feast of Ingathering" (Exo. 34:22, etc.) because it was the final fall harvest of all remaining nuts, fruits and any additional grain. It was also called "the Feast of Booths" because it was associated with Israel's wilderness journey and their dwelling in booths of foliage for some forty years (Lev. 23:40–43). The most common name for this Feast was another name for booths, which was "Tabernacles." This last is the most common designation we use today (Lev. 23:34 and Deut. 16:16).

### *The Feasts—God's Timetable*

Now, an important consideration for us to make regarding these Feasts is that they served as a *timetable or calendar* of supreme significance. The whole liturgical calendar of the nation of Israel was centered around the celebration of these three Feasts. They are called the "Pilgrimage Feasts" because on these three occasions the Israelites were to travel to appear before God. They were certainly of cultural significance to the mutual fellowship of the families of Israel. Most importantly, however, they are also designated by God as the *mo'adim*, *mowed* or *moed*, meaning "the *APPOINTED TIMES* of the LORD" (Lev. 23:4, NASB). This is the literal translation of the Hebrew word *moed* (see the *NASB Exhaustive Concordance*). It means *an appointment, a fixed time or season*, and is sometimes translated as a feast or festival in new translations. However, the literal translation is most important. God had stipulated this calendar of celebration for the nation of Israel as a very important memorial of things to come. Remember that the apostle Paul stated that the Hebrew Festivals and special Sabbaths were "a mere *shadow* of things to come" (Col. 2:16, 17).

In actuality, aside from the regular seventh day Sabbath observance, there were seven *mo'adim*, "Appointed Times," in Israel's liturgical calendar (see Lev. 23)—

1. The Passover Sacrifice (on the 14th day of first month).
2. The <u>Feast</u> of Unleavened Bread (15th-21st day of first month).
3. The special Wave-sheaf Offering of Firstfruit (on the day after the Sabbath).
4. The <u>Feast</u> of Firstfruits, Weeks or Pentecost (50 days later).
5. The Day of Trumpets (*Shofar*, 1st day of 7th month).
6. The Day of Atonement (*Yom Kippor*, 10th day of 7th month).
7. The <u>Feast</u> of Ingathering, Tabernacles (*Sukkat*, 15th-22nd day of 7th month).

Notice that only three of these "appointed times" are actually designated as *chag,* or *haggim,* the literal word for Feast or Festival. Most of our modern Bibles do not make this clarification. Some of those translations which do are *The Holy Scriptures, A New Translation*, by the Jewish Publication Society of America, 1917; their new version of 1962; *The Pentateuch & Haftorahs,* with Commentary, using the 1917 edition above; the *Emphasized Bible,* by Rotherham and the *New American Standard Bible*.

*"Three times you shall keep a Feast to Me in the year"* (Exo. 23:14). This is not merely a series of Feasts for the benefit of the people of Israel, but they were Feasts "TO GOD." And again, "Three times a year all your males shall appear *before the Lord God"* (Exo. 23:17). Again, "Three times a year all your males shall appear *before the LORD your God* in *the place which He chooses"* (Deut. 16:16). When we come to the inspired Greek Scriptures and observe the applications which the apostle Paul made from aspects of these Feasts, we will recognize a similar *timetable or calendar* for the subject of the resurrection of the righteous "to appear before God." Before we investigate this more carefully, we must take note of verses 21 and 22 here in 1 Corinthians 15.

## *The Two "Adams"* (Verses 21 and 22a)

After speaking of Christ as the "Firstfruit of those who have fallen asleep" in verse 20, Paul also directed our attention to Christ as prefigured by the first man, Adam, in verses 21 and 22. In these verses Paul compared two men—Adam and Christ. Through the first *"man"* (Adam) came death. Through another *"Man"* (Christ) came the resurrection of the dead. Everyone vitally connected to the first *"Adam"* is dying. Every man vitally connected to *"Christ"* is going to be resurrected from the dead or *"made alive."* Obviously, those connected to this second *"Man"* are going to experience the redemption of all that was lost by being connected to the first *"man."* Since all the unbelieving wicked are headed for what the Bible calls *"the second death,"* they are not included in the blessings of the resurrection of the righteous; they are not said to be *"in Christ."* Paul will later continue this theme in verses 45–49 of this same chapter. It will further confirm to us that the resurrection of these second and third "orders" is the resurrection of the *"just"* unto *"life,"* and does not involve the resurrection of the *"unjust"* unto *"damnation."* The resurrection of the wicked, being properly labeled *"the second death"* (Rev. 20:11–15), should not be expected to have any involvement in the resurrection that is before us—which is the resurrection of those *"in Christ"* and unto *"life."*

Later, in verses 42–49 Paul spoke of the natural bodies we have received from our physical forefather, *"Adam."* Those bodies are said to be "in corruption," "in dishonor," "in weakness," "a natural body" and "of the dust." In contrast to this, the righteous will be raised in bodies that we will have received from the *"last Adam"* (Jesus Christ). The new bodies which are guaranteed to us in Christ are described thusly, "in incorruption," "in glory," "in power," "a spiritual body" and "heavenly." Consequently, when Paul made reference in the earlier verses we read (verses 20–22) to the resurrection in the *"Man . . . Christ,"* it is to be understood that he was talking about the same resurrection of the righteous in glorified bodies as he later described in verses 42–49. This is further confirmation of the fact that the following "orders" of the resurrection of the dead only concern the saved who are said to be "*in Christ*." The unjust and unsaved are never said to be "*in Christ*." This will again be emphasized in the last part of this verse 22.

### "*In Christ* Shall All Be Made Alive" (Verse 22b)

The words "*in Christ*" are both inclusive and exclusive words. Only the saved are said to be "in Christ." The lost or unsaved are never said to be "in Christ." Four times in this chapter Paul used the expression "in Christ" and once, "in the Lord." In each and every case the expression means the very same people, the righteous by faith in Christ—see verses 18, 19, 22, 31 and 58. In addition, it is to be understood that all the righteous of all the ages are safe *in Christ*, Who is the basis for the salvation of all. Those in the times of the Hebrew Scriptures looked forward to Christ. We, who are living after the time of Christ's earthly sojourn, look backwards to Christ for salvation.

Earlier, in verses 18 and 19, Paul said that if Christ, Himself, had not been raised from the dead, then all those who have fallen asleep "*in Christ*" have perished and are "*most miserable.*" However, since it is an established fact—attested to by many witnesses and by the evidences which Paul gave—that Christ was raised from the dead, then we have the confidence that all who are said to be "*in Christ*" will also be made alive. Therefore, the words "*in Christ*" are given in verses 18 and 19 in answer to the possible frustration that would result if Christ, Himself, had not been raised from the dead.

Now verse 22 immediately before us is talking about the very same people as verses 18 and 19. Paul's designation is consequently very specific as to the fact that he was talking only about the resurrection of the righteous. So now we actually have additional confirmation that Paul was herein exclusively talking about the resurrection of the righteous. There will be no unsaved or unrighteous in any of these "orders." We can say that the Holy Spirit has, therefore, made this very, very clear in this passage. It is important that this conclusion be observed because there are many interpreters of this passage of Scripture who carelessly mingle the resurrection of the lost with the last of these "orders" of the resurrection of those "in Christ." That mistake will only bring confusion to the simplicity that is before us.

So, I will say again, and with the confirmations before us, that the following "orders" of this resurrection in verses 20 through 28 have nothing whatsoever to do with the resurrection of the lost. The resurrection of the lost is an entirely different event, with entirely different bodily conditions, and entirely different eternal consequences. It should never be mingled with the resurrection of the righteous which is the whole subject in this text.

### "But Each One *In His Own Order*" (Verse 23)

Another crucial word that the apostle Paul used in this section is the Greek word *tagma* which is translated "*order.*" This particular word is used only one time in the Greek Scriptures and that is right here in 1 Cor. 15:23. This means that the word is different or somewhat unusual. The lexicons all say that it is a military term which means a "company, or body of soldiers." As Paul used the word in this statement, "each in his own order," it means a series of "companies or bodies of troops" each following the other as if marching in rank. Now this word is used in the Greek Septuagint translation of the Old Testament. There it is used of the tribes of Israel as camped by "*rank and army in standard*" in Numbers 2:2 and as a "*troop*" in 2 Samuel 23:13. So there we have good illustrations of how it is used. The various Greek Dictionaries endorse this meaning:

Strong—"Something orderly in arrangement (a troop), i.e. (fig.), a series or succession."

Thayer—"That which has been arranged, thing placed in order. Spec., a body of Soldiers, a corps . . .1 Cor. 15:23 where Paul specifies several distinct bands or classes of those raised from the dead." By use of the word "*several,*" Thayer implies more than two "orders."

W.E. Vine—"That which has been arranged in order, was especially a military term, denoting a company; it is used metaphorically in 1 Cor. 15:23 of the various classes of those who have part in the first resurrection."

W. E. Vine is very accurate when he says, *"the first* resurrection" because the first resurrection involves only the righteous and not the unsaved.

> A Greek-English Lexicon, Arndt & Gingrich— "A military term for bodies of troops in various numbers such as divisions or battalions of soldiers . . . . In 1 Corinthians 15:23 the gift of life is given to various ones in turn, and at various times. One view is that in this connection Paul distinguishes three groups: *Christ,* who already possesses life, the *Christian,* who will receive it at His second coming, and *the rest of humanity . . .* who will receive it when death, as the last of God's enemies, is destroyed." (Italics mine, J. L.)

Now it is true that there are "three groups" intended in this series. However, the major difference I have from this last stated position by Arndt & Gingrich is that I am proving that the third "order" is most certainly not *"the rest of humanity,"* but the rest of *"the righteous dead,"* i.e., all the Old Testament and Tribulation saints who will be raised at the coming of Christ to rule and reign at the beginning of the Millennial Kingdom. The rest of humanity will be raised to damnation and not to life. Death is not "destroyed" for the unrighteous. Rather, it is an instrument in their damnation; therefore, their resurrection is called "the second death" (Rev. 20:14).

Henry Alford, in the English version of *Alford's Greek New Testament,* called *The New Testament for English Readers, A Critical and Explanatory Commentary,* gives a thought provoking statement (Vol. 3, page 1075):

> The three ranks are *mentioned in order of priority,* but this does not constitute their distinctive character: Christ is the *firstfruits*—this is His own rank, see Col. i.18:—*they that are Christ's* follows at His coming, who are the *lump* (as understood by the context, and implied by the term *firstfruits*), in the proper and worthiest sense, made like unto Him and partaking of His glory; then (after how long or how short a

time is not declared, and seems to have formed no part of the revelations to St. Paul, but was afterwards revealed —see Rev. xx. 4–6: . . .) shall come THE END, viz. the resurrection of the rest of the dead, . . . [All italics are his.]

By the use of the word *"lump,"* Alford is making reference to the specific term used of the Church of Jesus Christ at least twice in the letters of Paul—Romans 11:16 and 1 Corinthians 5:7 (see also 1 Cor. 10:17). This term is also a reflection back to the batch of dough used on the Day of Pentecost in making the two loaves of bread to be offered (Lev. 23:17). The statement in Romans 11:16 makes the connection very clear—"For if the *firstfruit* [the Wave-sheaf] is holy, the *lump* [for the two loaves of bread] is also holy. . . ."

Alford clearly delineates *three* orders to the resurrection of the righteous. However, as we shall see, Paul's qualifying statements in the passage do relate to the beginning of the Kingdom time period. In addition, Alford seems to equate the third "rank" or "order" not only with the saints mentioned in the "First Resurrection" of Rev. 20:4–6, but also "the rest of the dead" of verse 5, which would be the lost. This would be inaccurate. The lost are resurrected a "thousand years" later. We shall see that all the Old Testament saints are included in this third "order."

## *"Afterward . . . Then"* (Verses 23 and 24)

Of equal importance in demonstrating the three "orders" are the next two words. Fitting with the word "order" are the adverbs which show succession—*"afterward"* and *"then."* The Greek words *"epeita"* (afterward) and *"eita"* (then) are used where sequence is in view. Both these words are employed here to signify a succession of events:

1. *"Christ the firstfruits,"*
2. *"afterward* [epeita—next in sequence] *those who are Christ's at His coming,"*
3. *"then* [eita—next in sequence] comes *the end, when, . . . death is destroyed."*

Identical language is used elsewhere in this epistle to illustrate this. 1 Corinthians 12:28 says, "God has set some in the church, first apostles, secondarily prophets, thirdly teachers, _after that_ ['*epeita*'] miracles, _then_ ['*eita*'] gifts of healing, etc." Again, right here in chapter 15, verses 5–7 say, "and that He [Christ] was seen of Cephas, _then_ ['*eita*'] of the twelve: _after that_ ['*epeita*'] He was seen of above five hundred . . . _after that_ ['*epeita*'] He was seen of James; _then_ ['*eita*'] of all the apostles."

The employment of these words gives clear confirmation to the fact that there are **THREE** "orders" to the resurrection of the righteous— "<u>Christ</u>" (No. 1), "_afterwards_ . . ." (No. 2), and "_then_ . . ." (No. 3).

Furthermore, it is important to remember, in sequences such as this, that the subjects of the sequence remain in the same nature or character, i.e., the various "gift" positions in the Church (1 Cor. 12:28), and those who have seen the resurrected Christ (1 Cor. 15:5–7). Similarly, here in the resurrection chapter of 1 Corinthians 15, verses 23 and 24, the first two in sequence, without controversy, constitute the resurrection of the righteous dead. It follows that the third "order" must be of the same nature or character, i.e., the remaining righteous dead in Christ who are not of the first two companies. To insert that the last order of the resurrection is that of the unrighteous who are destined to damnation is to get everything "out of order" and in disarray, to say the least. By no stretch of the imagination are Christ and His Church to be placed "*in rank*" with the unrighteous who are marching to Hell! I will emphasize again— do not allow any teacher to confuse for you the two distinct kinds of resurrection, being that of the saved and the unsaved, with the three "orders" of the resurrection of the righteous.

I think I have demonstrated and proven conclusively that there is the "*Threefold* Order of the Resurrection of the Righteous." The contextual evidence and language construction clearly demonstrate that there are three "orders, companies or ranks" to the resurrection of the righteous. Having observed and demonstrated this, there is really no reason why any purported Bible teacher should not recognize it.

Now let us explore each of these three "orders."

## Chapter Three

# THE FIRST "ORDER"

### 1. "Christ The Firstfruit" (Verse 23a)

This is the first "order" of all those "in Christ" to be "made alive" (v. 22). It is properly and specifically Christ, Himself, as the "Firstfruit" of "those who have fallen asleep" (v. 20). It is noteworthy however, that though Christ's resurrection is primarily in view, yet in the "Firstfruit Wave Offering" there was a bundle of stalks of grain waved up in the air, not just a single stalk of grain. And indeed, there were others who were resurrected from the dead at the time of Christ's resurrection. Matthew tells us that when Christ died on the cross there was a great earthquake and "many of the graves were opened." After Christ's resurrection these saints came out from those graves and "appeared to many" in the city of Jerusalem (Matt. 27:51–53). Thus, there was a sufficient number resurrected at that time to fulfill the picture of a bundle of grain stalks waved in the air in the figure of the grain offering.

Though the law for this particular offering was revealed in Leviticus 23:9–14 during Israel's wilderness journey, yet they obviously could not perform it until they had arrived in the Land of Promise. In their wilderness journey there were no grain fields. When they came into the land we call Palestine, they inherited many grain fields and became farmers of the land. This special offering added an agricultural flavor to the whole Passover event, and made it the first of what came to be called "The Three Agricultural Feasts" of Israel: one, Passover or Feast of Unleavened Bread; two, Pentecost or Feast of Weeks; and three, Tabernacles or Feast of Ingathering. The "Offering of the Omer," or the Sheaf to be waved in the air during this first Feast, served as the token of the greater spring harvest to be celebrated seven weeks later on the fiftieth day.

The law of Leviticus 23:10–11 stated—

> Speak to the children of Israel, and say to them: 'When you come into the land which I give to you, and reap its harvest, then you shall bring a *sheaf of the firstfruits* of your harvest to the priest. He shall shall wave the sheaf before the LORD, to be accepted on your behalf; on the day after the Sabbath [which occurs during the Feast of Unleavened Bread] the priest shall wave it.'

The spiritual significance or meaning of the "Firstfruit Offering," originally offered on a Sunday morning at the time of the resurrection of Christ, is the following:

1. The initial planting of the seemingly dead kernels of grain serves as a picture of *death*. Christ said as recorded in John 12:24, "Most assuredly, I say unto you, *unless a grain of wheat falls into the ground and DIES,* it remains alone; *but if it DIES*, it produces much grain."
2. The springing up of the new stalks of grain and their harvesting in the spring speak of the new life and their *resurrection from the dead*. Christ said ". . . *it produces much grain*" (John 12:24). The apostle Paul explained—"But someone will say, 'How are the dead raised up? And with what body do they come?' Foolish one, what you sow is not *made alive* unless it dies. And what you sow, you do not sow that body that shall be, but mere grain—perhaps wheat or some other grain. *But God gives it a body as He pleases,* and to each seed its own body" (1 Cor. 15:35–38). How beautiful and strong this

argument is! Whenever one is in the countryside and looks out on the abundant fields of new grain, it should be remembered that all this sparkling new *life* came out of what appeared to be *death*—cold, hard kernels planted into the ground, awaiting the moisture and sun rays by which they would spring to life and be *raised up.*

3. The ritual harvesting of the first sample of grain and its offering to God speak of Christ's resurrection as the "Firstfruit" (Lev. 23:10) *sample* and *guarantee* of those to be raised from the dead (verse 23). Christ promised that in His death He would *"produce much grain"* (John 12:24). And again, the divinely inspired apostle Paul left no doubt in one's mind as to the meaning—"Christ is risen from the dead, and has become the Firstfruits *of those who have fallen asleep"* (1 Cor. 15:20). And then for emphasis Paul repeated the truth again—*"Christ the Firstfruits, . . ."* (verse 23). Some other passages which represent this *guarantee* of the believer's resurrection are: (1) Ephesians 1:13, 14, "In Him you also trusted, after you heard the word of truth, the gospel of your salvation; in Whom also, having believed, you were sealed with the Holy Spirit of promise, Who is the *guarantee* of our inheritance until the redemption of the purchased possession, to the praise of His glory"; (2) 2 Corinthians 5:5, "Now He Who has prepared us for this very thing [the resurrection of the body] is God, Who also has given to us the Spirit as a *guarantee*"; (3) Romans 8:11, " But if the Spirit of Him Who raised Jesus from the dead dwells in you, He Who raised Christ from the dead will also give life to your mortal bodies through His Spirit Who dwells in you."

4. As we have seen so far, this typology is clearly identified as a picture of Christ in *resurrection.* However, Christ was not just raised from the dead. He also *ascended up* into the heavens to His Father. Thus, what happens as a major action with this particular offering is the manner in which it is offered. In the ritual offering, the grain is not burnt on the altar, nor is it spilt out beside the altar or sacrificed in any way. It is not placed in any pots or pans. It is not merely held out by the hands.

Rather, the Sheaf is waved up in the air as if God would reach down and take it. This waving of the grain up in the air is said to be done *"before the LORD"* (Lev. 23:11). In other words, it is intended to picture going up to God. It belongs directly to God in heaven. The *waving up in the air* of the bundle of grain to the Lord speaks visually of Christ's ascension up to God. Christ reminded Mary Magdalene in these words, "Do not cling to Me, for I have not yet *ascended* to My Father" (John 20:17). Sometime after Christ's resurrection was the spectacular event of His ascension up into heaven to the Father. (See John 20:17; Luke 24:50–51; Acts 2:32–35; Eph. 4:8, 9 and Psalm 68:18.)

5. The Wave-sheaf or handful of grain ("Omer") stood primarily as a token or guarantee of the greater harvest to be **celebrated fifty days later**. So vital was this connection that they, therefore, *counted the days and weeks* which followed (Lev. 23:15, 16) until the Pentecostal spring harvest Feast. Some Jewish commentators even call "Shavuot" (the Feast of Weeks or Pentecost) *"the eighth Day of the Feast of Unleavened Bread"* precisely because of its vital connection to the Offering of the Omer. This special offering stands, therefore, as the *token* "Firstfruits," a *guarantee* of the whole spring "Harvest Feast of Firstfruits" yet to come.

### *The Timing of the Offering*

As to the exact timing of this offering, it is not at all accidental that Christ in His resurrection fulfilled it perfectly. In my book, *The Day Christ Died As Our Passover*, I demonstrate conclusively that Christ perfectly fulfilled the chronology of events in the Passover services. He was selected on the "tenth day" of Nisan, which in the Gospel accounts is described as His triumphal entry into Jerusalem on the Sunday before Passover. This was the day, according to the original Passover in Egypt, on which the lambs or goats were to be selected (Exo. 12:3). In addition, contrary to Christendom's "Good Friday" memorial, Christ was sacrificed in the afternoon of the 14th day of Nisan (a Thursday) on the "Preparation Day" at the precise time the Passover lambs were being sacrificed in the Temple area (Matt. 27:62; Mark 15:42; Luke 23:54 and John 19:42). The four Gospels, likewise, make it very clear that Christ was resurrected from the dead early on Sunday morning, the first day of the week (Matt. 28:1; Mark 16:1; Luke 24:1 and John 20:1). That would mean that the offering of the Wave-sheaf, which typified His resurrection, was also offered on that morning.

However, the Devil always wants to bring confusion to biblical reality. As to the specific day upon which this "Offering of the Wave-sheaf of Firstfruits" should be made, there was a dispute between the Pharisees and Sadducees of first century Judaism. The interpretation of the timing of this offering, as spelled out in the Law of Moses, was the subject of heated controversy in those early rabbinic times. No doubt this needs to be explained because in Jewish custom today this "Offering of the Omer" is rarely ever celebrated on a Sunday morning. This incongruity stands as an obstacle to believing the harmony of Gospel accounts with apparent Jewish law or custom today.

The historical record tells us that before Christ was born, the Sadducees came into authority and prevailed in controlling the priesthood and the order in the Temple services. They continued to hold control until about 20 years before the destruction of the Temple by the Romans in A.D. 70. Thus, the Sadducees directed the Temple services during the time of Christ's death, resurrection and the establishment of early Christianity (see Acts 4:1 and 5:17). Politically, the Sadducees were in good standing with the Roman authorities during that time. In addition, many people do not realize that the "Offering of the Omer" under their direction was always on a Sunday morning. It was during the last 20 years of the Temple that the Pharisees gained control and many things changed, including the day upon which the "Omer" was offered. Their tradition has prevailed until this very day.

It has been well-known that the Sadducees were very liberal in their beliefs and rejection of certain fundamental truths, such as a literal resurrection of the dead and the existence of angels, spirits, etc. (see Luke 20:27–38; Acts 4:1–2 and 23:8). However, they were also surprisingly conservative and literalists in aspects of interpreting the Law. In fact, they held that only the Law (the first five books of the Bible) was to be regarded as divinely inspired. In addition, they very firmly rejected the various traditions of the Pharisees. Though the Pharisees were highly orthodox, yet they went even beyond the Law to observing their "Oral Law" (traditions) as equal authority as the written Law. Their oral traditions sometimes contradicted the written Law. This is one reason Christ rebuked the Pharisees so severely. This was the major difference between the two groups, and it was the major difference in the observance of the timing of the "Offering of the Omer" (the Wave-sheaf of Firstfruits). This difference had to do with the particular "Sabbath" intended, after which the Wave-sheaf was to be offered.

The instructions in the Law of Leviticus 23:10 and 11 read—

> . . . you shall bring a sheaf [omer or handful] of the Firstfruits of your harvest unto the priest. He shall wave the Sheaf before the LORD, to be accepted on your behalf; on *the day after* the *Sabbath* the priest shall wave it.

### "The Day after the Sabbath"

Now the meaning of *"the day after the Sabbath"* on which the Pharisees would observe the offering eventually prevailed in practice after they had gained control of the high priesthood and the Temple services. They took it to mean the "High Sabbath" of the first day of the Feast of Unleavened Bread. This tradition still prevails in Judaism to this very day. In addition, this custom actually makes the Sunday morning resurrection of Christ, according to the four Gospels, appear to stand in contradiction to Jewish custom. In other words, if Christ's resurrection was typified by the Wave-sheaf Offering, then His resurrection would NOT have happened on a Sunday morning because that would not be the day after the "High Sabbath" of the first day of that Feast. Sunday morning is not the normal time of that offering in present Jewish custom.

It is a fact, according to the Law of Moses, that there were two kinds of Sabbath days. There was the regular seventh day Sabbath which all observed throughout the year. This would always be on a Saturday. In addition, the Law mandated special "High Sabbaths" to be observed. These were in relation to the Feast celebrations and the observance of the *High Days* of "the blowing of the Shofar" (Trumpets) and "Yom Kippur" (the Day of Atonement). There were actually seven of these High Sabbaths—*two* during the Feast of Unleavened Bread (one at the beginning, the 15th day, and one at the end, the 21st day), *one* for the Feast of Pentecost, *one* for the Day of Trumpets, *one* for the Day of Atonement, and *two* for the Feast of Tabernacles (one on the 15th day, and one on the 22nd day). This made seven High Sabbaths in all.

Now, according to this present Jewish custom, stemming from the tradition of the Pharisees, the Sabbath after which the Offering of the Omer was to be made was the "High Sabbath" of the first day of the Feast of Unleavened Bread. This High Sabbath was always on the 15th day of the month, no matter what day of the week it was. This meant that the Offering of the Omer would always be on the morning of the 16th day of the month which was rarely on a Sunday. At the time of Christ this High Sabbath was on Friday, the first day of the Feast of Unleavened Bread. Saturday morning would be when the Offering of the Omer was to be made according to Pharisaic tradition.

However, as I stated before, at the time of Christ's death and resurrection, the Sadducees were still very much in control of the Temple services and the priesthood. They rejected this attempt of the Pharisees to change the timing of this offering.

The tradition of the Pharisees on this subject actually stemmed from their effort to assign some historical event in Israel's early history to the celebration of the Feast of Pentecost (Feast of Firstfruits). To them, the Feast of Shavuot (Pentecost) seemed to stand disconnected to anything in Israel's early history. Passover was obviously attached to Israel's deliverance from Egyptian bondage. Sukkat (Tabernacles) was also assigned to represent Israel's 40 year wandering in the wilderness. But there seemed to be nothing with which to connect Shavuot (Pentecost). This Feast was only identified by the number of weeks (Shavuot) and days (50) from the Offering of the Omer.

A casual look at Israel's early travels out of Egypt, as recorded in the book of Exodus, indicates that it took them approximately

50 days to reach Mount Sinai where the Law was given. So the Pharisees chose to assign Pentecost or Shavuot as a commemoration of the giving of the Law from Mount Sinai. They went backwards to the day of the Exodus, which was the 15th of Abib (later, Nisan) as the starting point for their 50 days, and also assigned this High Sabbath as the day preceding the Offering of the Omer.

Therefore, historians believe that the Pharisees took this position in order to correlate the Feast of Pentecost with the giving of the Law of Moses. In the biblical account this is not at all stated, nor is there any later history in the biblical record of Israel to indicate that they believed this or observed this tradition.

The Sadducees, on the other hand, rejected this attempt to change the nature of Shavuot which was to them simply connected with the first harvest theme. In addition, they rejected the time the Pharisees wanted to have the Offering of the Omer. The Sadducees took the passage in Leviticus very literally and thus, since the word "Sabbath" was not designated or specified as the "High Sabbath," it would be the regular Seventh Day Sabbath which would fall during the Feast. Consequently, the Offering of the Omer would always be on a Sunday morning—and so it was at the time of Christ's resurrection from the dead.

At the time of Christ, this meant that on Sunday morning when the priests were making this particular Wave-sheaf Offering before the LORD in the Temple services, the disciples were hearing the almost unbelievable news of Christ's resurrection from the dead. Christ's resurrection was exactly on God's predetermined schedule and no amount of satanic confusion would change this glorious fact. In addition, the Roman soldiers frantically rushed away from the tomb to confer with the priesthood as to their experience at the tomb. The soldiers, as the Gospel account tells us, were offered bribes and special protection to give a false account of what had actually happened at the tomb (see Matt. 28:11–15).

So it was, that the liberal Sadducees, who did not believe in the physical resurrection of the dead, stood in the Temple services this very unusual Sunday morning, probably with mixed emotions. Some had, no doubt, already heard the report from the Roman soldiers and now faithfully turned their attention to *wave up in the air* the

Sheaf of Firstfruits as God had prescribed in the Law. Thus they executed, exactly on *schedule*, the very ritual which demonstrated and announced the *resurrection of Israel's Messiah*. And, perhaps some of them even then, if not later, remembered the words of Christ to them a few days earlier, "For He [God] is not the God of the dead but of the living, . . ." (Luke 20:38). God's Word never returns void—see Acts 6:7.

Many scholars today agree with the understanding of the Sadducees on this matter. The historical references for this material are taken from:

1. *The Pentateuch & Haftorahs*, edited by J. H. Hertz, under "the Omer," pages 520, 521;
2. *The Encyclopedia Judaica*, under "Sadducees" and "Shavuot";
3. *Guide to the Jewish Holy Days* by Hayyim Schauss, pages 87, 88;
4. *Davis Dictionary of the Bible*, under "Weeks, Feast of," page 809;
5. *The Jerusalem Post, International Edition*, articles by Rabbi Reskin, "What's in a name?" June 1, 2006, and "Something doesn't add up," May 21, 1999 (and the June 6, 2003 article).

*Chapter Four*

# THE SECOND "ORDER" (A)

## 2. *"Afterward Those Who Are Christ's"* (Verse 23b)

The second reason I realized Paul was most certainly using the symbolism of the three Harvest Feasts of Israel as the backdrop for the threefold order of the resurrection of the righteous is because of the exact terminology he employed in this second *"order."* Paul did not say, "afterwards the Church" or "afterwards the saints of this age of Grace." Those designations may very well have been accurate as to the group of saints of which he was speaking, but that is not the wording Paul was inspired to use. It is important to realize that the wording Paul used is designed to *connect* those resurrected in this second order directly *to Christ*, and to what Christ, Himself, *represented*. Christ is clearly and specifically the "Firstfruit" of those to be raised from the dead. That means that Christ's "Firstfruit" resurrection is the representation of the "Firstfruit Harvest" to come later. It follows, therefore, that the second group to be resurrected will be identified in substance as *belonging to Christ* and to what Christ *represented*. "Afterwards those who *are Christ's*" is, therefore, the exact wording which attaches this group to Christ. Consequently, it must be descriptive of the spring "Harvest of Firstfruits" which eventually followed Christ's resurrection from the dead and would be celebrated some 50 days later at Pentecost.

In this regard, *The New Bible Commentary: Revised,* by Eerdman's Publishing Co., (page 1071) makes the following excellent observation, "First fruits implies *community of nature* with the 'harvest' to follow; i.e., Christ's *resurrection* promises the ultimate *home-gathering* of all God's people. The full harvest was foreshadowed and consecrated by the first sheaf brought as an offering." (Italics mine, J. L.)

Now there are two important statements in this observation made in *The New Bible Commentary: Revised.* The first point I am making here is that Paul's statement, "Those who are Christ's," is demonstrating a *"community of nature."* Since Christ was the "Firstfruit" sample, this must be the "Firstfruit Harvest." The second important statement is "Christ's *resurrection* promises the ultimate *home-gathering* of all God's people." This means the Harvest Feast of Pentecost actually symbolizes *resurrection* or *"home-gathering."*

The dedication of the whole Harvest of Firstfruits at Pentecost was signified by the consecration of the Firstfruit Wave-sheaf at Passover. The Sheaf is the first sampling of the whole harvest to come. By this act of the dedication of the Wave-sheaf sampling, they were in effect consecrating the whole harvest to the Lord God. Consequently, at the time of Christ's resurrection there was the *Wave-Sheaf Offering* presented before the Lord. Likewise, at the time of the celebration of the whole harvest fifty days later, there was the *Wave-loaves Offering*, also presented before the Lord. Both offerings are vitally connected and each symbolized **resurrection and ascension.** In like manner, according to the principle stated by Paul in Romans 11:16—*"For if the Firstfruit* [Christ] *is holy, the Lump* [the Church] *is also holy."* What the one is, so is the other! In actuality, therefore, the Feast of Firstfruits (Pentecost) is the clear fulfillment of Christ's words as recorded in John 12:24—"Unless a grain of wheat falls into the ground and dies, it remains by itself alone; but if it dies, it will *bring forth* [by resurrection] *much grain* [in resurrection]."

### The Feast of Conclusion

In this connection, one of the additional names for this particular Feast, which I have not previously mentioned, is "The Feast of

*Conclusion*" (Heb., *Hag ha-Azereth*, or simply *Azereth*). This was the rabbinic name given to the Feast of Pentecost because of its close association to the offering of the Wave-sheaf during the Feast of Unleavened Bread. This close connection between the two offerings is demonstrated several ways: (1) by the *"counting of days and weeks"* from one to the other; (2) by the similarity in the designations of both by the term *"Firstfruits,"* the one the *sample*, and the other the *harvest*; (3) by the similarity of both being *grain offerings* and (4) by the similarity in the manner of both being *"waved"* up in the air before the Lord. Therefore, the rabbis considered it as a "one day addition" to the Feast of Unleavened Bread for seven days, just as there was a one day extension to the Feast of Tabernacles. Tabernacles was a seven day Feast with an eighth day culmination celebration added (Lev. 23:36 and Num. 29:35). Therefore, the words "Afterward those who are Christ's" carries the idea that is expressed in this other name which is given to the Feast—*"The Feast of Conclusion."* As to the spiritual significance of the first Offering being the *resurrection* of Christ, so it must follow that the major spiritual significance of the second Offering is the *resurrection* of "those who are Christ's," as well! Of course, the grand and blessed *"Conclusion"* to Christ's resurrection is the resurrection and/or the Rapture of the Church belonging directly to Jesus Christ!

The word "firstfruits" by itself simply has reference to the first harvest of grain in the new year. The early "Sheaf of Firstfruits," waved in the air during the Feast of Unleavened Bread, was simply the token and dedication of the whole "Harvest of Firstfruits" to be celebrated 50 days later at Pentecost. Whatever Pentecost must typify, it must typify the *resurrection* of the saints precisely because the Pentecostal Offering gets its character directly from the Wave-sheaf Offering during Passover.

Furthermore, as Henry Alford also pointed out (page 1075, of his material quoted earlier), there is a similarity of words here in 1 Corinthians 15 with Paul's language employed in 1 Thessalonians in describing the Rapture of the Church. The statement earlier (1 Cor. 15:20) that Christ is the *"firstfruits of those who have fallen asleep"* has clear reference to Christ being the firstfruits of *"those who sleep in Jesus*" as stated in 1 Thessalonians 4:14. In addition, the statement here in 1 Corinthians 15:23, "*those who are Christ's,*" is the same as "*the dead in Christ*" in 1 Thessalonians 4:16. And also the words, "*at His coming,*" in 1 Corinthians 15:23 are the same as Paul's words ". . . *the coming of the Lord*" in 1 Thessalonians 4:15. In other words, "*then those who are Christ's*" has clear reference to the Rapture of the Church as Paul first revealed in 1 Thessalonians 4. So it is that the Rapture of the Church is in view in this second "order" of the resurrection of the righteous. The parallel wording and the parallel truth between 1 Corinthians 15:20 and 23 with that of 1 Thessalonians 4:14 and 16 is inescapable.

I don't know of any reason one would disagree with this basic conclusion. Even Robert Gundry, in his book *The Church and the Tribulation*, agrees that there are at least two orders to the resurrection of the righteous, and that this second order involves the Church saints (see page 148). However, he contends that this resurrection event takes place after the Great Tribulation. Furthermore, he states that there is no third "order" clearly indicated. (The publishers of his book believe that his book would become the "standard text on the posttribulational viewpoint of the Rapture of the Church.") Of course, he is clearly mistaken in this conclusion—there is a third "order"! I have already given what several lexicons state about there being "three orders" to the first resurrection. In addition, I have already demonstrated the facts of the specific Greek terms used for three "orders." This information was long available to Robert Gundry. In addition, as we go further, I will demonstrate that it is the third "order" which takes place after the Great Tribulation, not the Rapture of the Church.

Now let us continue to discuss this second "order."

### *"New Grain Offering"* (Lev. 23:16)

Fifty days after the offering of the Wave-sheaf of Firstfruits was the offering of the two loaves of bread (made by preparing enough dough for two loaves) at the "Feast of Firstfruits" (Heb., *Hag Habikurim*). As stated earlier, this Feast is most often called the "Feast of Weeks" (Heb., *Shavout*) or "Pentecost" (Greek, 50th).

The offering from the mixture of dough, which was in the form of two loaves of bread, is called the *"New Grain Offering"* in Leviticus 23:16. It is undoubtedly a fact that the spiritual meaning and explanation of this particular offering lay dormant in Israel's history until the time of the revelations given to the apostle Paul concerning the *"One New Man"* (Eph. 2:15), which is also called *"One Bread"* (1 Cor. 10:17).

I realize that there are a few conservative Bible teachers who very surely believe in the pretribulational Rapture of the Church, but do not believe that any application of these Feasts of Israel should be made to the Church. No doubt, there have been many careless teachers who go to what has been called "the Fall Feasts" and try to assign some significance from them to the Rapture of the Church. This has only brought confusion because these "Appointed Times" in the fall season of Israel's calendar, most certainly, do not apply to the Church. It is also true that there are no open and direct prophecies in the Hebrew Scriptures concerning the Church. It was indeed "a mystery hidden in past ages" (Eph. 3:1–7). Consequently, no one expected the Church or the Age of Grace. However, scriptural typologies are not necessarily in the same category as direct and open prophecies. Often the typology itself does not come to open perception until the reality has been clearly established. As these typologies may apply to the Church, once the reality has come, then one can look back and see things never realized before, which previously never had any typical meaning. Earlier this truth, just as the reality, was hidden in the typology.

Yet some continue to reason that since the Church of Jesus Christ was described as a "mystery not known in past ages" (Eph. 3:1–5), therefore, the Church could not be typified by anything in past ages. Again, I would agree with this logic unless, that is, as I just stated, the typologies in the Hebrew Scriptures concerning the Church were themselves "mysteries" unknown until God brought them to light, just as He does the Church. I intend (the Lord willing) to devote a chapter in a coming book (*The Pentecostal Rapture of the Church*) to deal more effectively and thoroughly on the subject of Pentecost being typical of the Rapture of the Church. I think the reservation by some on this point is an extremely cautionary move, and yet unnecessary, especially when we see all the relevant truths about Pentecost and certain aspects of the Church being typified in the Hebrew Scriptures. Remember, also, that the unique feature of this age as a time of Gentile salvation was well-known by the prophets. I will discuss more of these features in this later book on the subject of the Rapture.

In addition, I would agree that none of the Feasts do apply to the Church, with the exception of this one very *unique Feast* which God, Himself, *vitally connects* to the birth of the Church of Jesus Christ. The Church of Jesus Christ was not only born on the Day of Pentecost; it was, in fact, created at the very moment when the time had *"fully come"* (Acts 2:1) of the Offering of the Wave-loaves. This is the very focal point of Pentecost. Alford Edersheim, the renowned Hebrew-Christian scholar, in his book *The Temple, Its Ministry and Services*, pages 266, 267, captures the moment in these words—

> For, as the worshippers were in the Temple, probably just as they were offering the wave-lambs and the wave-bread, the multitude heard that 'sound from heaven, as of a mighty rushing wind,' which drew them to the house where the apostles were gathered, there to hear 'every man in his own language' 'the wonderful works of God.'

Thus the exact historical facts of the Church's precise birth at about 9 A.M. in the morning (Acts 2:15), which was also the understood time of that vital morning offering, inescapably identify the "New Grain Offering" with the creation of "the One New Man" (Eph. 2:15) of this Age of Grace. In addition, we shall see that both the work of Holy Spirit directly and some additional spiritual truths from the apostle Paul are most surely vitally connected with this Feast.

### *"The One New Man"* (Eph. 2:15)

This One New Man, "the Church which is Christ's body," actually began on the Day of Pentecost. Pentecost is the birthday of the Church. Most interpreters agree with this. (Of course, there are

49

those extreme dispensationalists who deny this fact and in so doing have caused no little confusion, especially among themselves. They say that what was created on Pentecost was a "Kingdom Church." They argue that the "Church which is Christ's body" did not come into existence until sometime later (?) during the ministry of Paul. Then they obviously end up having two churches or "bodies" in existence at the same time during the Acts period time frame.) There actually should be no doubt that the spiritual significance of Pentecost points to the Church of Jesus Christ which was uniquely created on that day.

It is interesting that those, who don't believe Pentecost could be typical of the Church, at least admit that Pentecost was typical of "the coming of the Holy Spirit" on the Day of Pentecost (see the paper by Thomas Ice, whom I highly regard, entitled *Israel's Fall Feasts and Date-setting of the Rapture*, with quotes from Terry C. Hubert's doctoral thesis entitled *The Eschatological Significance of Israel's Annual Feasts*).

Yes, after denying that Pentecost could refer to the Church and affirming that all the Feasts only have reference to the nation of Israel, it just so happens that in this thesis Hubert states that the real significance of Pentecost was "the coming of the Holy Spirit." Now, this admission on his part is actually deadly to his conclusion that it does not have reference to the Church! Certainly he must realize that the Holy Spirit at Pentecost was the Holy Spirit Who "baptizes all believers into one body, the Church which is Christ's body" (see Acts 1:5 with 1 Cor. 12:13 and Eph. 1:22, 23). Thus the Holy Spirit at Pentecost, by this very baptism, initially created the Church. In addition, this is the same Spirit Who restrains the appearance of Antichrist until "He (the Spirit) is taken out of the midst" (2 Thess. 2:7). Furthermore, it is the same Holy Spirit Who guarantees the resurrection of the Church (Rom. 8:11). Thus it becomes obvious that "the Holy Spirit of Pentecost" is the Holy Spirit Who was promised by Christ (John 14:15–18) to lead His Church and Who uniquely characterizes the whole life of this present Age of Grace. This is clearly NOT the Holy Spirit's work in His distinct function relative to the nation of Israel! So, obviously, Pentecost becomes directly related to the Church, whether one likes it or not. It seems to me that on this subject Mr. Hubert may have gained his doctorate, but he certainly "talked in circles" about the significance of Pentecost.

Even to this time Jewish teachers are only speculative as to the meaning of Pentecost. Amazing as it may seem, Shavuot or Pentecost has even been spoken of as a "**mystery**" feast (see *The Jerusalem Post, International Edition,* June 1, 2006, "*What's In A Name*" by Rabbi Reskin). As I pointed out earlier, it was only in post biblical times that the Pharisees officially assigned the giving of the Law for a purpose in the celebration. That God has now in the Greek Scriptures made manifest the spiritual explanation of Pentecost will become more clear as we compare Romans 8:11 and 23 with 1 Corinthians 15:23. Likewise, in several other passages, Paul showed how the Church's resurrection is vitally connected to that of Christ's resurrection (see 1 Thess. 4:14; 1 Cor. 15:20; Rom. 8:11, etc.). There is no doubt that "*Those who are Christ's*" (1 Cor. 15:23) is the same as "*the dead in Christ*" (1 Thess. 4:16) who will rise first.

### *"Firstfruits of the Spirit"* (Rom. 8:11 and 23)

Not only was Paul saying by positive inference in 1 Corinthians 15:23 that the next "order" in the resurrection of the saints is the "Harvest of Firstfruits," but that is explicitly what he said in Romans 8:11 and 23. Thereby we have confirmation that the Church of Jesus Christ is represented by the "Firstfruit" harvest. Listen to Paul's words:

> But if the *Spirit* of Him Who *raised Jesus* from the dead *dwells in you*, He Who raised Christ from the dead will also *give life to your mortal bodies* through His *Spirit* Who dwells in you . . . And not only this, but we also ourselves, having the **firstfruits** *of the Spirit*, even we ourselves groan within ourselves waiting eagerly for the adoption as sons, *the redemption of our body*. (Italics and bold mine, J. L.)

Thus, the members of the Church of our Lord Jesus Christ are specifically identified as having the "*Firstfruits of the Spirit*" in anticipation of their ***resurrections from the dead***. This fits perfectly with Paul's second "order" of those raised from the dead (1 Cor. 15:23). Consequently, one could arrange 1 Corinthians 15:23 in the following manner in order to reflect the truth of Romans 8:11 and 23 upon it:

> But each in his own order:
> *Christ the firstfruits* [demonstrated by the
>         Wave-sheaf Offering at Passover],
> *Afterward those who are Christ's*
>         [having the **firstfruits** of the Spirit and
>         demonstrated by the Wave-loaves Offering
>         at the Feast of Firstfruits, i.e., Pentecost],
>         at His coming.

No one argues that the token "Firstfruit" is other than Jesus Christ. This is what the text very plainly says twice (verses 20 and 23). Likewise, no one should argue that Christ's resurrection was not the immediate token and guarantee of the resurrection of the Church of Jesus Christ. Many Scriptures connect the resurrection of Christ as the basis for the resurrections of the members of the Church. And now, as to God's timetable, the Church was both born on the Day of Pentecost and is symbolized by the special offering of the two Wave-loaves at this Feast. In addition, the members of the Church are specifically said to possess the "Firstfruits of the Spirit" in anticipation of their bodily redemptions. Consequently, there is no doubt that the second "order" in this resurrection sequence is plainly demonstrated to be that of the Church of Jesus Christ.

Of additional importance is the fact that this means there must be a separate and distinct "order" of resurrection exclusively for the Church! Of necessity, it also follows in sequence that there must be a separate and distinct "order" to accommodate the resurrections of the Old Testament and Tribulation saints! We shall investigate the biblical revelation about the resurrection of the Old Testament saints shortly.

### *Firstfruits in Resurrection*

Let us herein review the scriptural and historical principles which identify and connect Pentecost with the theme of resurrection.

1. The Offering on the Day of Pentecost receives its character directly from the Offering of the Firstfruits during the Feast of Passover. The prophetic character of the Wave-sheaf Offering sample made during the Feast of Passover admittedly symbolizes the *resurrection* of our Lord Jesus Christ. Consequently, the prophetic character of the Wave-loaves made at the Feast of Pentecost must have reference to *resurrection* as well. The Firstfruits Sheaf was itself prophetic of **resurrection** concerning the Firstfruits Harvest.

2. In consistency with this, here in 1 Corinthians 15:23 Paul was, in effect, directly saying, "Christ is the Firstfruits [in *resurrection*], then they that are Christ's," meaning the Firstfruits harvest is the next "order" in **resurrection**.

3. The Offering on the Day of Pentecost was even more vitally connected back to the offering of the Wave-sheaf as emphasized by other facts regulating the observance of Pentecost. One cannot date Pentecost until the earlier date of the Wave-sheaf Offering is established. Days and weeks are carefully counted off from one to the other, intimately connecting them in anticipation. The counting of days begins with the first until the fiftieth. This means that the Wave-loaves at Pentecost are in effect the *conclusion* of the Wave-sheaf at Passover. As we saw, in Jewish custom Pentecost became known as the Feast of Conclusion—*Hag ha-Azereth*. What greater "conclusion" could there be than the **resurrection** connection?

4. In Romans 8:11 and 23 Paul made the connection twice. In verse 11 he told the Church saints that they have the same Holy Spirit in them Who raised up Christ from the dead, and that, consequently, the Holy Spirit would perform the very same **resurrection** in them. In addition, in verse 23 Paul stated that the Church has "the Firstfruits of the Spirit" in anticipation of their bodily resurrections. What does this mean? It simply means that the principle established by Christ's resurrection

from the dead—as the "Firstfruits" of those "who sleep in death"—is now vitally connected to us by the Holy Spirit, so as to constitute the Church as being the Firstfruit Harvest in regards to the *resurrection* of our bodies:

> But if the Spirit of Him Who raised Jesus from the dead dwells in you, He Who raised Christ from the dead will also *give life to your mortal bodies* through His Spirit Who dwells in you. . . . but we also who have the *Firstfruits Of the Spirit*, even we ourselves groan within ourselves, eagerly waiting for the adoption, *the redemption of our body.*

5. As pointed out by Henry Alford, the similarity of words and truth as expressed between Paul's statements in 1 Corinthians 15 and 1 Thessalonians 4 is inescapable—

   (1 Cor. 15:20) Christ is the "firstfruits of *them that sleep.*"
   (1 Thess. 4:14) "God will bring with Him *those who sleep in Jesus.*"

   (1 Cor. 15:23) "*those who are Christ's.*"
   (1 Thess. 4:16) "*the dead in Christ* will rise first."

   (1 Cor. 15:23) "*at His coming.*"
   (1 Thess. 4:15) "*. . . the coming of the Lord.*"

So, there should be no question that the second "order" in 1 Corinthians 15:23 is the Rapture of the Church as described in 1 Thessalonians 4. In addition, this second "order" in the resurrection of the righteous corresponds perfectly with the second Harvest Feast on God's timetable. Pentecost has become the Church's day in this regard. It is also the beginning of the unique time of Gentile salvation and "outcalling."

I believe we will see even more beautiful evidences of this as we progress further in this study.

## Chapter Five

# THE SECOND "ORDER" (B)

### *The Wave-loaves at Pentecost*

Fifty days after the offering of the "Wave-sheaf of Firstfruits" at Passover is the offering of the "Wave-loaves" at the "Feast of Firstfruits," also called "Pentecost." The spiritual significance of this offering is the following:

1. The planting of the seeds in the fall served as a picture of death, or more appropriately, of those who are said to have *"fallen asleep"* in Christ;

2. The selected ripened stalks of grain being harvested for this special offering speak of the *resurrection* from the dead of the whole spring harvest;

3. A *"New Grain Offering,"* as it is designated by the Spirit of God, speaks of the Church of Jesus Christ as a *"New Creation"* (2 Cor. 5:17) or *"One New Man"* (Eph. 2:15);

4. However, this grain is not offered in its raw state, but is ground into fine flour and kneaded together in one batch, speaking of the members of the Church as being totally assimilated into one entity—i.e., *"By one Spirit are we all baptized into one body"* (1 Cor. 12:13), being *"one bread"* (1 Cor. 10:17);

5. "Baked" speaks of being tried and tested. The leaven can actually speak of the Church's rapid growth into a wholesome food. Though leaven is often used to symbolize evil, this does not necessarily always follow;

6. The large batch of dough divided into two loaves simply speaks of double fruitfulness. (Some interpreters think this may mean Jew and Gentile. However, in the Church the Jew and Gentile are all mingled together in the one batch);

7. The *"waving up in the air"* speaks of ascension (Rapture) up into heaven, even as it did in the case of Christ as the "Wave-sheaf";

8. To be presented *"before the Lord"* speaks of the Church's collective gathering in heaven before Christ and God;

9. Accompanied by the various blood sacrifices, all of which speak of this special offering being done on the basis of the total, finished work of Christ as our Savior;

10. The number 50 simply signifies **fullness** or **completion**. In seven days God *completed* His work of creation (Gen. 2:1, 2). 7 X 7=49, with the celebration on the next day=50, signifying *perfect completion* or *fullness*. As stated by E. W. Bullinger, the number 50 "points to deliverance and rest following as the result of the *perfect consummation of time*." (*Number In Scripture*, by E. W. Bullinger, page 268; italics mine, J. L.) As with the celebration of the Jubilee on the 50th year (see Lev. 25:8–13), so it is with Pentecost in terms of 50 days. In this regard, it is noteworthy that an allusion to the Jubilee 50th year release and the "Firstfruits" of Pentecost are blended together in Romans 8:18–23. There Paul speaks of the "liberty" from bondage of the curse in the physical creation waiting until the resurrection of the saints who have the "Firstfruits of the Spirit."

### *Fullness or Completion*

The common translation of Acts 2:1 is "When the Day of Pentecost had *fully come*, . . ." (All the italics in these verses are mine, J. L.). Actually, this translation in itself gives further confirmation to the fact of *fullness* and *completion* being the meaning expressed by the number 50 and the word, "Pentecost." We can also note that a more literal translation of Acts 2:1 is "When the Day of Pentecost was *completed*" (see *The NASB Interlinear Greek-English New Testament*). Another very literal translation was made by Alford which reads—"while the day of Pentecost was being *fulfilled*." And yet another rendering by Rotherham in his *Emphasized Bible* states, "And <when the day of Pentecost was *filling up* [the number of days]>. . ." Now these translations in their renderings all place the emphasis upon the fact that the "counting of days" had been *completed*. The seven weeks or full forty-nine days have passed and the fiftieth day has arrived. And this is actually what the Greek word used here is saying—*sumpleroo*, which is a compound word; *sum*, meaning "**completely**," and *pleroo*, meaning "**to fill**." Together it means "*to fill completely*." This also gives us the spiritual significance or meaning of the numeral 50 as used in the Law; it simply speaks of "*fullness or completion*."

In addition, the Greek word *pleroo* (or *pleroma*) is used on two other occasions where the apostle Paul applied it to this present dispensation of time. First, Paul was inspired to connect the word "fullness" (*pleroma*) with the conclusion of this age (Rom. 11:25) of the "out-calling of Gentiles" (Acts 15:14). Note these two verses in sequence—

> Acts 15:14; Simon [Peter] has declared how God at the first visited the *Gentiles to take out of them a people for His name.* Romans. 11:25; For I do not desire, brethren, that you should be ignorant of this mystery, lest you should be wise in your own opinion, that blindness in part has happened to Israel until the *fullness* [*pleroma*] *of the Gentiles has come in.*

Though the early Church began among the Jewish people, yet one of the unique characteristics of this present age is that it quickly evolved into a primary time of salvation for the Gentile people. National Israel, in carnal rejection of her own Messiah, became "set aside" till a future time of restoration. In turn, the gospel was eagerly received among the Gentile nations of the earth. Now Paul is revealing here in Romans that when God has "filled completely" that "calling out of Gentiles," then Israel will again be restored into a place of favor with God.

Since Pentecost is actually prophetic of the future resurrection and ascension of the Church, then it follows that when the "fullness or completion" (50th) of the out-calling of the Gentiles comes, which characterizes the Church in this age, then the antitypical Pentecost— or the prophetic aspect of Pentecost—will be "completed." This is when the Age of Grace will have come to a close. Therefore, Paul's words could be understood as saying, "When the antitypical *Pentecost* comes, this Age will be completed."

In addition, Paul was inspired to describe this whole dispensation of time by the word *pleroma*. In Ephesians 1:10, he stated—

> . . . that in the Dispensation of the *Fullness* [*pleroma*] *of the Times* He [God the Father] might gather together in one all things *in Christ*, both which are in heaven and which are on earth—in Him.

Some dispensationalists understand this to be a reference to the future Messianic Kingdom Age. However, I remember an older minister, whom I highly respected, who looked at this passage with intensity, and then said to a group of us that he highly suspected that this statement by Paul is actually a reference to Christ's exalted position in the present Church Age. And indeed, when one looks at the later context, Paul did explain the dynamics of the present position of Christ at the right hand of the Father (verses 17–23). Furthermore, when one compares a similar statement made by Paul in Colossians 1:18–20, it will become obvious that this is a description of this present Age:

> And He is the head of the body, the Church, Who is is the beginning, the firstborn from the dead, that in all things He may have the preeminence. For it pleased the Father that in Him all the *fullness* [*pleroma*] should dwell, and by Him to reconcile all things to

Himself, by Him, whether things on earth or things
In heaven, . . .

Here in Colossians Paul gave the same basic statement which is clearly describing Christ's preeminence in the present Church Age. In the case of Ephesians 1:10, the correct interpretation is, therefore, that Paul characterizes this whole Church Dispensation as *"the Dispensation of the Fullness of Times."* This is similar to saying that the present Church Age can be called *"The Pentecostal Dispensation."*

In this regard, we can now realize that: (1) not only did Pentecost mark the *beginning* or birthday of the Church (Acts 2:1, 2), (2) but Pentecost also has ingredients which characterize the *totality of the Church's dispensational character* (Ephesians 1:10) and finally (3) Pentecost, as to its numerical value, even looks forward to the very *fullness of the Church's members* on the earth (Romans 11:25).

This becomes an amazing revelation pertinent to the Church's connection to what Pentecost prefigured! Actually, the surprising thing about this is that most scholars and Bible teachers today have missed the full implications, even though all have suspected some vital connection.

### Resurrection and Rapture of the Church Passages

Direct references to the resurrection and Rapture of the Church are only to be found in the Greek Scriptures, primarily in those epistles written by the apostle Paul. This will by no means be a full listing of all the references of this great hope since there are so many. However, I will list the most significant ones which demonstrate the uniqueness of this resurrection "order" for the purpose of this Bible study. Later I will list those references from the Hebrew Scriptures which spell out the anticipation of the future resurrection of the Old Testament saints. You will notice an exceptional difference between the passages from the Hebrew Scriptures and these from the Greek Scriptures.

There are three important facts which everyone should notice concerning the passages from the Greek Scriptures. *First,* there will be the clear statements concerning the resurrections of the dead with immortal bodies. The *second* important fact is that LIVING SAINTS who are alive at the end of this Age will also be glorified, having also received immortal bodies. And the *third* fact is that the resurrected, glorified dead along with the glorified living saints will both *"together"* be *"caught up"* (raptured) to "meet Christ in the air." Now these last two important facts are never stated of the resurrection of saints in the Hebrew Scriptures. The saints of the Hebrew Scriptures simply expected to be resurrected and go alive into the Messianic Kingdom on earth, whereas the saints of this second "order" are promised a specific "heavenly" hope. In fact, Paul will specifically say *"the hope which is laid up for you in heaven, . . ."*— Colossians 1:5.

Two passages make it very clear that in the resurrections of those belonging to the "Church which is Christ's body," the sudden disappearance of living saints all over the world (because the Church of Jesus Christ today includes all saved people all over the world) will take place. As I stated before, this was never stated of those to be resurrected from Old Testament times.

| | |
|---|---|
| 1. 1 Thessalonians 4:15–17 | For this we say to you by the word of the Lord, *that we who are alive and remain* until the coming of the Lord will by no means precede those who are asleep. For the Lord Himself will descend from heaven with a shout, with the voice of an archangel, and with the trumpet of God. And the dead in Christ will rise first: *then we who are alive and remain* shall be *caught up together* with them *in the clouds to meet the Lord in the air.* And thus we shall always be with the Lord. |
| 2. 1 Corinthians 15:51–52 | Behold, I tell you a mystery: *we shall not all sleep,* but we shall *all be changed*—in a moment, in the twinkling of an eye, at the last trumpet. For the trumpet will sound, and the dead will be raised incorruptible, *and we shall be changed.* |
| 3. Colossians 1:5 | . . . *the hope which is laid up for you in heaven,* of which you heard before in the word of the truth of the gospel. |

4. Philippians 3:14    I press toward the *goal for the prize* of the *upward call* of God in Christ Jesus.

5. 1 Thessalonians    For what is *our hope*, or joy, or crown of
   2:19              rejoicing? Is it not even you *in the presence of* our Lord Jesus Christ at His coming?

6. 2 Thessalonians    Now, brethren, concerning the coming of our
   2:1               Lord Jesus Christ and *our gathering together to Him*, . . .

7. John 14:2–3       In My Father's house are many mansions; if it were not so, I would have told you. *I go to prepare a place for you.* And if I go and prepare a place for you, *I will come again and receive you to Myself;* that *where I am, there you may be also.*

In light of all that we have read earlier in the previous passages that I have listed (and many others as well), our remembrance returns to what Christ privately told the apostles on the night of His betrayal and awakens us to the reality of which He spoke. The elements of what Christ said above in John 14 are all parallel to all these verses we have read. Christ was resurrected from the dead here on this earth, and then He ascended into heaven. There He is preparing places for the saints who are to follow Him. In turn, He will come again to receive them as in the Rapture of 1 Thessalonians 4. Then He will take them into heaven to the prepared places. The similarity is undeniable. In addition, there is a remarkable parallel in other respects between 1 Thessalonians 4:13–18 and John 14:1–3.

8. 2 Thessalonians    . . . for that day will not come unless *the departure*
   2:3 and 2:7, 8    *comes first*, and the Man of Sin is **revealed**, the son of perdition, . . . For the mystery of lawlessness is already at work; only He [the Holy Spirit] Who now restrains will do so until *He is taken out of the way.* And then the lawless one will be **revealed**, . . .

For a long time I have resisted using this passage because it has been argued by some (see again *The Church and the Tribulation,* by Gundry, pages 115–117) that the Greek word *apostasia* is never used in the Scriptures, including the Greek translation of the Hebrew Scriptures called the Septuagint, other than as a "defection from the faith." This is stated even though the basic meaning of the word is admittedly *"departure,"* and the major Greek Lexicon by Liddel and Scott (*A Greek-English Lexicon*) gives "departure or disappearance" as the secondary meaning when not used in a "religious" sense.

First of all, though it is true that in the cases in the Septuagint where the word is used in the clear context of religious defection, it is always properly translated as *defection* or *apostasy.* Yet I have found that the *Concordance of the Septuagint* by Morrish does list where the exact Greek word *apostasia* means a simple "departure" of a person from a location and not a defection or apostasy. In 1 Kings 20:13 (in the Septuagint; 1 Sam. 20:13 in the NKJV) Jonathan told David that he could *"depart (apostasia) in peace, and the Lord shall be with thee. . . ."* So here is what seems to be an illustration or example of what Liddel and Scott said in the Greek Lexicon of the secondary use of this word.

And that means that here in 2 Thessalonians, it is the contextual evidence which becomes most important in determining the use of this word. In this case, the context certainly does not directly indicate a particular religious departure from Christianity, nor does it indicate a religious departure from Judaism. The "Man of Sin" herein mentioned is certainly described as a "lawless one" who brings in a flood of iniquity. However, he is never described as an apostate Jew or an apostate Christian. He would more surely fit the description of an infidel, atheist or agnostic who suppresses all religion—except the worship of himself. In addition, in this passage Paul says this *"apostasia* (Greek) comes first," so it would not be the "lawlessness" brought in by the "Man of Sin," himself.

Also, in this case the "departure" of the Church and the *"Man of Sin being revealed"* (verse 3) fit perfectly the Holy Spirit being "taken out of the midst" so that the *"lawless one will be revealed,"* as stated in verses 7 and 8.

Therefore, I am prone to believe that "the departure" mentioned here by the apostle Paul is indeed that "disappearance" of the collective "body of Christ."

## The Timing of Pentecost

Most Bible teachers in recent times have placed the emphasis upon Pentecost as simply being "the birthday of the Church." They have either forgotten all about, or else did not realize, what the Wave-loaves ritual actually symbolized by (1) its *harvest nature*, (2) its *connection to the Firstfruit sample* at Passover, (3) the action of *harvesting*, (4) the *waving up* of the offering and now (5) the *timing* of the Offering.

For a moment let us go back to the Firstfruit Offering during the Feast of Unleavened Bread. There is no mistaking by anyone what the Wave-sheaf Offering of the Firstfruit symbolized in *substance*— which was the resurrection of Jesus Christ! In addition, Christ was risen from the dead as a *sample* and *guarantee* of the greater resurrection harvest to come. As to the *action* of the harvesting of the offering, all recognize that the seemingly dead kernels springing to life prepictured the bodily resurrection of Christ from the dead. Then the waving of the Sheaf up in the air prepictured His *ascension* up to the Father in heaven! Also, as to the *timing* in the typology, the ritual was fulfilled exactly on schedule by the Sunday morning event. This was true in spite of the Pharisaic intent to change the timing of that beautiful occurrence. The Wave-sheaf typology was actually fulfilled by Christ's resurrection from the dead at that very time.

Now in a similar way, we have the whole harvest of wheat celebrated 50 days later in an amazingly *identical manner*, so it must also symbolize the same theme of resurrection from the dead. This must be the primary feature of Pentecost. However, about the only thing modern teachers realize is the symbolism of the two loaves of bread as being typical of the Church. What about the Church's RESURRECTION FROM THE DEAD? And what about its ASCENSION UP TO HEAVEN? And what about the symbolism as to the TIMING of that event? Of course, it must be true that as the first Sheaf sampling of grain offered represented resurrection, so the Two Loaves of Bread also represent RESURRECTION FROM THE DEAD—the Two Loaves of Bread representing the fruit of the full harvesting of the living and ripened grain field. And again, the waving of the Loaves of Bread up in the air must symbolize the very same thing as the waving of the Sheaf of Firstfruits did earlier—ASCENSION—in this case, the ascension of the Church UP TO HEAVEN! In other words, to say it very plainly, the offering at Pentecost actually prefigures the Rapture of the Church of Jesus Christ! There is no escaping the conclusion of the divinely prescribed typology. We must now realize that Pentecost is actually one of the most solid scriptural prophecies by typology of the Rapture of the Church.

Lest anyone doubt this, allow me to further point out that the Greek word *harpazo*, which is translated "caught up" in 1 Thessalonians 4:17 concerning the Church of Jesus Christ, is the identically same word used of the ascension of Jesus Christ as portrayed in the vision of John in Revelation 12:5—

> She [Israel] bore a male Child Who was to rule all
> nations with a rod of iron. And her Child was *caught
> up* [*harpazo*] to God and His throne.

Of course, many know that the Greek word *harpazo* is the word from which we get the translation of "Rapture." Consequently, we can scripturally realize that as Christ was Raptured (Rev. 12:5), so will the Church also be Raptured (1 Thess. 4:17). This is strong confirmation to the fact that the *Wave-sheaf Offering* prefigured the exact same event as does the *Wave-loaves Offering* on the Day of Pentecost—i.e., the Rapture of the Church.

Last, but not least, we must return to the question—what about the *timing* of this great event? Herein most Bible teachers hold their breath and are squeamish about the Rapture of the Church taking place on an actual Jewish Feast day, the Day of Pentecost as prescribed in the Jewish calendar—and they absolutely should be!

However, I do not believe that the Church is to be Raptured on an actual *calendar day* of the Pentecostal Feast Day. Some have thought so and, I must admit, at one time I was mistakenly one of them. Nevertheless, I do surely believe, after careful and consistent study which I am demonstrating in this book, that the Church will be Raptured on the Day *symbolized* or *prefigured* by Pentecost. I have found that Pentecost is the only Feast day in Israel's liturgical calendar, concerning all its Feasts and Appointed Times, *which does NOT demand a prophetic fulfillment on a precise calendar day!* In other words, this is the only Feast which can typify the Church of Jesus Christ *and yet NOT cause one to fall into the trap of date-setting!* Nor does it violate the doctrine of imminency in the expectation of Christ's coming for His own.

Remember, I said earlier in this study that one of the most unusual things about this Feast is that Pentecost was not attached to anything in Israel's historical beginning as were the Feasts of Passover and Tabernacles. Its only identity was in the *number 50*. That very fact, that Shavuot was only designated by the counting of days and weeks until the 50th day was reached, is what caused the Pharisees to try and attach the Feast of Pentecost to the giving of the Law from Mount Sinai. And now, like the Pharisees of old, the one thing we should not do is to try to attach Pentecost's fulfillment to anything in Israel's history—not even the *calendar day* of the Pentecost Feast, itself. This is most important to remember, for if it is attached to any specific date, such as the calendar Day of Pentecost, itself, then we make null and void the fact that the Rapture of the Church is to be expected at any moment. The Rapture event is always pending and is not designated to occur on any revealed date. It is certainly imminent to every generation of believers. What, then, is the timing of the antitypical Pentecost?

Remember that Pentecost stands "parenthetical" between the Feasts of Passover and Tabernacles, and was primarily known only by the counting of days. Its prophetic fulfillment would be determined by what the number 50 *symbolizes* in Scripture. Therefore, and consequently, since the number 50 simply symbolizes *"Fullness or Completion,"* then we can definitely know for certain that when the *"Fullness or Completion"* comes in God's divine estimation, this is when the typology of Pentecost's prophetic timing will be fulfilled! The Church will be suddenly "caught up to meet Christ in the air." It should be quite obvious to all that God alone knows and determines when the "Fullness of the Gentiles," which is the antitypical 50$^{th}$, will have arrived.

So it is that the Rapture of the Church will indeed occur on Pentecost—but NOT on the calendar Day of Pentecost which stood as the "birthday" for the Church. Rather, that eventual Pentecost, *"fullness* and *completion,"* as symbolized by the Feast Day, i.e., "when the *fullness* of the Gentiles has come in" (Rom. 11:25).

## Chapter Six

# THE THIRD "ORDER" (A)

### 3. *"Then the End, when . . . Death is Abolished"* (Verses 24–26)

Here is the third "order" of the resurrection of the righteous. As the first two "orders" were distinct from each other, so this "order" is distinct and separate from each of them. This means that the previous resurrection of the dead, which was the resurrection and Rapture of the Church, is to be regarded as distinct and separate from the resurrection which will now follow at the "end." As we shall see, this last "order" is the resurrection of all the Old Testament and Tribulation saints. In this resurrection there is no change or glorification of living saints and there is no Rapture of these saints up into the air towards a heavenly hope (Col. 1:5).

Many are puzzled (and for a long time, I was one of the many) about this last order of the resurrection in this particular passage of Scripture. By now you may be tired of reading that this has nothing whatsoever to do with the resurrection of the unjust at the final termination of the earth after the Millennial Reign of Christ. However, I have needed to emphasize this because so many interpreters of this passage erroneously suppose this symbolizes the resurrection of the *unsaved* at the end of the Millennium. This error would be similar to saying that at the final Feast of Israel all the Jebusites, Philistines, Canaanites, Hittites, Perizzites and Amorites would appear before the Lord instead of the Israelites. This would not be in proper "order," but in chaos. This last grouping would not fit into the divine typology of these Feasts. Moses never ordered any collective gathering for the pagan idolaters. All three Feasts and all three *"orders"* are to be attended by the people of God—nobody else. There are simply three stages in which all the righteous will appear before God in resurrection, "the resurrection of the just."

There is another, final, important reason why we can know that this third *"order,"* wherein *"death is abolished,"* could not possibly be talking about the resurrection of the wicked. The resurrection of the wicked or unjust is specifically identified as *"the Second Death"* (Rev. 20:6 and 12–14). In other words, Death is NOT *Abolished* in the resurrection of the unjust. There is certainly a resurrection—but not to Life! For the lost, Death is not an *enemy* to be destroyed, but rather an *instrument* in the hands of God to punish them. They will be brought back into physical existence, but that existence will be in eternal "Death" and separation from God. This "Death" will never be destroyed (Rev. 20:10–15).

Now our attention can be drawn to this third "order." We shall see that there is one important difference in this last "order" of the resurrection of the righteous in comparison to the first two "orders." As to the Feast symbolism, in this "order" there will be no *"Wave Offering up to God"* as there was with the previous two "orders." Rather, we shall find that these saints will be resurrected to go immediately into the Millennial Kingdom *on earth* to directly assist and rule on earth. They will not be transported into heaven as was Jesus Christ, and as will be the Church of Jesus Christ.

## *Resurrection of Old Testament and Tribulation Saints*

In the Hebrew Scriptures, and also several times in the Gospel accounts, there is very plainly stated the fact of the resurrection of the righteous from the state of death. This has reference to all the saints who died, from Adam until the Day of Pentecost in Acts chapter 2. Generally speaking, these passages will always relate the resurrection of the Old Testament saints to the time of the second coming of Jesus Christ to reign on earth after the Great Tribulation.

In addition, sometimes the exact timing of that resurrection is clearly indicated. The reference in the book of Revelation (20:4–6) will also specify the saints of the Great Tribulation in this resurrection. We will go over these following references very carefully and note in particular the time indicated for this resurrection:

1. Job 19:25–27      For I know that my Redeemer lives, *and He shall stand at last* [lit., at the end] *on the earth*; and after my skin is destroyed, this I know, that in my flesh shall I see God, Whom I shall see for myself, and my eyes shall behold, and not another. How my heart yearns within me!

The book of Job was an account which took place just before the time of Abraham. To realize that God's saints from early times knew of their future resurrection from death is very sobering. God did not hide this truth from them, but they fully embraced it and "yearned" for that time to come. Notice, of course, that Job's resurrection will take place when his Redeemer "*stands at last on the earth.*" This is in obvious contrast to the Rapture of the Church to meet Christ "in the air." For Job there will be no "meeting in the air." At that time Job will look upon God the Son on this earth. This is a reference to the time of the second coming of Christ when He shall reign on earth.

2. Isaiah 25:6–9      And in this mountain the LORD of hosts will make for all people a feast of choice pieces . . . And He will destroy on this mountain the surface of the covering cast over all people, and the veil that is spread over all nations. *He will swallow up death forever*, and the LORD will wipe away tears from all faces; the rebuke of His people He will take away from all the earth . . . And it shall be said in that day: 'Behold, this is our God: we have waited for Him, and He will save us. This is the LORD; we have waited for Him; we will be glad and rejoice in His salvation.'

The context here is "the mountain" of the LORD'S house in Israel as stated in Isaiah 2:2. This is where Christ will return at His second coming and will there deliver Israel. This represents the saints waiting for the Messiah on earth. Likewise, at that time *"death is swallowed up"* for the dead saints of the Hebrew Scriptures time period.

Now some have concluded that since Paul quoted this principle of *"death being swallowed up"* in 1 Corinthians 15:54 in connection with the Rapture of the Church, that this resurrection event spoken of in Isaiah 25 is the same as, and will take place at the same time as, the Rapture of the Church which is specified in 1 Corinthians 15:50–55. This is a very hasty conclusion. It is a fact that the principle of *"death being swallowed up in victory"* was first demonstrated at the resurrection of Jesus Christ from the dead, but no one takes that to mean that the resurrection of Christ takes place at the same time as the resurrection of all the Old Testament saints. So it is, that *"death will be swallowed up"* is true in principle of the Rapture of the Church, just as it is of the Old Testament saints. By no stretch of the imagination does this mean that the Rapture of the Church is the same as this last "order" of the resurrection of the righteous. The whole purpose of Paul is to distinguish these "orders." This is a distinct "order" of the saints at the very "end" time.

3. Isaiah 26:19–21     *Your dead shall live; together with my dead body they shall arise. Awake and sing, you who dwell in dust;* for your dew is like the dew of herbs, *and the earth shall cast out the dead.* . . . For behold, the Lord comes out of His place to punish the inhabitants of the earth for their iniquity; . . .

As was true of the previous passages, this glorious event of the resurrection of the dead shall take place at the second coming of Christ to rule and reign on the earth. Specifically, the resurrection takes place at the time Christ comes to "punish the inhabitants of the earth for their iniquity."

4. Daniel 12:1–3 . . . and there shall be a time of trouble, such as never was since there was a nation, even to that time [the Great Tribulation]. And at that time your people [Israel] shall be delivered, everyone who is found written in the book. *And many of those who sleep in the earth shall awake, some to everlasting life,* some [at the end of the Millennium] to shame and everlasting contempt.

It is again obvious that this "awakening" of the dead shall happen when Daniel's people, Israel, "shall be delivered" at the end of the "time of trouble, such as never was." This is a reference to the Great Tribulation and therefore specifies the time of the deliverance of Israel and the "awakening" of "those who sleep in the dust of the earth." This is the time of the resurrection of all the Old Testament saints.

5. Daniel 12:12, 13 Blessed is he who waits, and comes to the one thousand three hundred and thirty-five days. But you [Daniel], go your way till the *end*; for you shall rest, *and will arise to your inheritance* at the *end* of the days [the days specified in verse 12].

This is an amazing revelation! Daniel's resurrection is specified as taking place at the "END," which is the very same terminology Paul used in 1 Corinthians 15:24—"then the END, . . ." In addition, the revelation to Daniel appears to specify "the end of the [1335] days" just mentioned in context. The 3 ½ years of the Great Tribulation is broken down in Scripture to equal "1260" days (Rev. 11:3 and 12:6). Add to this an additional 75 days after the Tribulation to equal the "1335" days of verse 12. This, then, is the time we come to when Daniel (and others) will "arise to [his] inheritance at *the end*."

6. Hosea 13:14 *I will ransom them from the power of Sheol; I will redeem them from death. O Death, I*

> *will be your plagues! O Sheol, I will be your
> destruction! . . .*

This statement is made in the midst of Hosea recounting the
story of Israel's continued apostasy through the history of the
nation. Hosea reminded them of the calls for repentance, beginning
at the time of their wilderness journey and continuing through the
time of their kings, and the consequent calamities which befell
them. But suddenly he was led to give this splendid assurance of
ultimate victory from both Hell and the grave or Death, itself. As a
*principle* this would be true of all the "orders" of the resurrection
of the righteous, including Christ, Himself. Therefore, the apostle
Paul also quoted it in conjunction with the Rapture of the Church in
1 Corinthians 15:54 and 55. Again, by no stretch of the imagination
does this mean that the resurrection of the Church and of the Old
Testament saints would happen at the same time. I say again, the
whole purpose of Paul in 1 Corinthians 15:20–28 is to differentiate
the *people* and the *timing* in the "orders" of the resurrection of the
righteous.

7. John 6:39, 40, 44,    . . . and I will *raise him up* at the last day. Martha
   54 and 11:24          said to Him, 'I know that he will *rise again in
                          the resurrection* at the last day.'

In these passages Christ simply stated that there is the resurrection
*"in the last day."* For all the saints who would die before the Church
began, this resurrection would be at the second coming of Christ to
earth to rule and reign. This would mean after the Great Tribulation,
as stated in the prophets. Were any of these people Christ addressed
to die in the Church dispensation, "the last day" would mean at the
Rapture. No doubt, in John 11:24, Martha (who spoke) was thinking
in terms of the time designated by the prophets.

8. Matthew 8:11      And I say to you that many will come from the
   and Luke 13:28    east and west, and sit down with *Abraham,
                      Isaac and Jacob* in the Kingdom of heaven.
                      There will be weeping and gnashing of teeth,

when you see *Abraham* and *Isaac* and *Jacob*
and all the *prophets* in the Kingdom of God,
and yourselves thrust out.

In these two passages Christ spoke of Abraham, Isaac and Jacob
being seen *"in the Kingdom of God,"* which is the same as the
Messianic Kingdom here on this earth. That being true, these saints
had to have been raised from the dead at the commencement of that
Kingdom. This indicates that all the saints of old will also be there.

9. Romans 11:15     For if their [Israel's] being cast away is the
                    reconciling of the world, what will their
                    acceptance be but *life from the dead?*

I do not know for certain whether or not this is an actual reference
to the physical resurrection of the saints or a figurative use of the
expression, "life from the dead." "Their acceptance" is certainly a
reference to the restoration of the nation of Israel into favor with
God once again. As we have seen thus far from the prophets, there
is a resurrection of the dead to take place when Israel is restored.
However, it has also been pointed out that the prophet Ezekiel
described the restoration of the nation of Israel in Ezekiel 37:1–14
in terms of the vision of the valley of dry bones, wherein the whole
nation would come to life again as if "life from the dead."

10. 1 Corinthians     Then *the end*, when . . . the last enemy that will
    15:24–26          be destroyed *is death* . . . for He must reign
                      till He has put all enemies under His feet.

This, of course, is the passage presently under discussion in this
Bible study.

11. Revelation     Then the seventh angel sounded: and
    11:15–18       there were loud voices in heaven, saying,
                   'The kingdoms of this world have become
                   the kingdoms of our Lord and of His Christ,
                   and He shall reign for ever and ever! . . .

73

> The nations were angry, and Your wrath has come, and *the time of the dead*, that they *should be judged*, and that You *should reward Your servants the prophets and the saints,* and those who fear Your name, small and great, . . .'

This certainly has reference to the judgment of the resurrected "dead" and the "rewarding" of the prophets at the time of Christ's coming to reign on earth over all the kingdoms of this world. This would be the Old Testament saints, not the Church.

12. Revelation 20:4-6

> . . . And I saw the souls of those who had been beheaded for their witness to Jesus and for the Word of God. . . . *And they lived* and reigned with Christ for a thousand years, . . . Blessed and holy is he who has part in the *first resurrection.*

Notice again, that this takes place at the end of the Great Tribulation and at the beginning of the thousand year reign of Messiah.

(Luke 14:14; 20:35–36 and Acts 24:15 are passages which simply state that there will be "the resurrection of the just," without identifying any of the "orders.")

When we thus read all these passages carefully, they make it very plain that all the saints living before the time of the present Church Age expected their resurrections to occur at the last day — at the time of Messiah's coming to deliver Israel and to rule on earth. The book of Revelation indicates this same resurrection (11:15–18), but primarily mentions those who have suffered martyrdom during the Great Tribulation in chapter 20:4–6. Actually, the passages from the book of Daniel appear to indicate that this resurrection will occur some seventy-five days after the conclusion of the Great Tribulation (see also my chart on *"The Future Week of Prophecy"* at the end of this study). We shall see that when the Messiah returns to earth, the first thing He will do is to destroy all earthly kingdoms and fight against His enemies. Then there will be a great cleansing for Israel. At that time the dead Old Testament and Tribulation saints shall be raised.

*Chapter Seven*

# THE THIRD "ORDER" (B)

### *"Then The End"* (verse 24)

The Greek word for "end" is *telos*. It simply means "end, termination, cessation, consummation, completion, last part, close or conclusion." In a few cases this word carries the idea of "fulfillment, aim, goal, purpose or outcome." Another radically different way in which it is used is in reference to the collection of "tax, customs or duties." It is derived from the word *"tello"* which means to "set out for a definite point or goal." However, this word *"tello"* is never used in the Greek New Testament, and *"telos"* rarely has that meaning (purpose or goal) in the Greek Scriptures. Thayer's Lexicon says "what 'end' is intended the reader must determine by the context." In a moment we shall see that the immediate context supplies us with the answer in terms of a quotation from Psalm 110:1, which is a clear prophecy about the second coming of the Messiah to rule and reign on earth in mighty power. In a similar way, it is also a fact that the word *"telos"* is most often used in description of the great last day event of the second coming of Christ at the *"end"* of the age (Matt. 10:22; 24:6, 13, 14; Mk. 13:7, 13; Luke 21:9; 1 Pet. 4:7 and Rev. 2:26). Paul also uses the word with reference to the *"end"* of the present age (1 Cor. 1:8; 10:11; 2 Cor. 1:13; Heb. 3:6, 14 and 6:11).

Interestingly enough, and also a "must" for our consideration, is the fact that the third and last Feast on Israel's sacred year calendar is said to be at the *"end"* of the year (Exo. 23:16, KJV). The Hebrew word for *"end"* here literally means *"the going forth or out."* It is most often translated in this case as *"the end of the year."* Exodus 34:22 also states that the Feast occurs at the *"course or turn"* of the year and is sometimes translated "at the *end* of the year," as well. Certainly it was the "end" of the agricultural seasons.

Furthermore, as I pointed out earlier, in the book of Daniel it is expressly stated that this resurrection will occur *"at that time* [the conclusion of the great time of trouble]" and "[you, Daniel] shall stand in your lot, *at the end of the days"* (Dan. 12:9 and 13). In fact, all the prophecies from the Hebrew Scriptures, concerning the resurrection of the saints of old, say that it will occur at this same *end time* event of Messiah's coming to judge and rule on the earth.

Thus it is, that both the time of the final "order" of the resurrection of the righteous and the final Feast of Israel employ the use of the word *"end,"* and supply us with the third reason why I believe Paul is using the symbolism of the Three Harvest Feasts of Israel as the backdrop for the three "orders" of the resurrection of the righteous.

### *"When He delivers the Kingdom to God,"*
Qualified by
### *"When He Abolishes all Rule, Authority and Power,"*
Qualified by
### *"For He Must Reign 'Until He Has Put All Enemies Under His Feet'"*
(Verses 24, 25 and Psalm 110:1)

In 1 Corinthians 15:24 the expression, *"Then the End,"* as it relates to the final resurrection of the just, has a series of qualifications as to when it will happen. It is first qualified by *"when He delivers the Kingdom to God."* However, "when He delivers the Kingdom to God" is itself further qualified by *"when He abolishes all rule, authority and power."* And finally, the *"abolishment of all rule, authority and power"* is itself explained by the events in Psalm 110 which Paul quoted. We could totally misunderstand when this *"end"* takes place were it not for Paul quoting this particular Psalm. This Psalm is one of the most often quoted passages in the Greek Scriptures (see Matt. 22:44; Acts 2:34, 35; Heb. 1:13; Heb. 10:13 and here in 1 Cor. 15:25).

When we read Psalm 110 we see clearly the basis for determining exactly "when" this "end" time event takes place. Quoting from the NASB (italics and bold mine, J. L.):

1. *The LORD said to my Lord: 'Sit at My right hand,*
   ***Until I make Thine enemies a footstool for Your feet.'***
2. *The LORD will stretch forth Your strong scepter from Zion,*
   *saying, **'Rule in the midst of Your enemies.'***
5. *The Lord is at Your right hand; He shall **shatter kings***
   ***in the day of His wrath.***
6. *He will judge among the **nations**, He will fill them with corpses,*
   *He will shatter the **chief men** over a broad country.*

It is clearly here in Psalm 110:1–6 that the Messiah will "*Abolish all Rule, Authority and Power.*" According to this Psalm the very first days of the rule of the Messiah will be done while He is "*in the midst of His enemies.*" In other words, at the very beginning of His reign He will be a warrior King doing battle with His enemies. It will be "*the Day of His Wrath.*" He will destroy armies, kings and governmental powers on earth. He will judge the nations of earth in wrath. According to the great image vision of King Nebuchadnezzar, the "Stone cut out of the mountain will smite the image in its feet," and the whole image will become "dust" (Dan. 2:24–45). There will be multitudes of slain. Thus, the *first work* of the Messiah is to subdue and destroy all God's "enemies."

Knowing the prophesied time of the resurrection of the saints of old, the apostle Paul added in this passage of 1 Corinthians 15 that "*The last enemy to be abolished is Death*" (v. 26). Therefore, when Death has been abolished and the saints of old are resurrected, "*all enemies* will have been placed under His [Messiah's] feet" (v. 25). "*All Rule, Authority and Power*" will have been abolished, including "*Death.*" And this is precisely "*when*" He victoriously "*delivers the Kingdom to God.*" Christ "*delivers the Kingdom . . .*

*WHEN He abolishes all rule* . . . [with] all *enemies* under His feet." Consequently, *"The delivering of the Kingdom"* is not left to our guesswork as to when it will be done. It is nowhere said to be done *after* He has reigned on earth for a thousand years. On the contrary, it will occur at *the very beginning* of His reign upon the destruction of all earthly powers and the resurrection of the saints of old.

Alford's *Critical Commentary on the New Testament* (pages 1075 and 6) makes the same observation. He states that at the point ". . . when it [the Kingdom] shall be fully established, every enemy overcome, everything subjected to Him, He will not [yet] reign over it and abide its King, BUT DELIVER IT UP TO THE FATHER." In further clarification, Alford observes that Christ, being "the mediatorial King," will "At this very time of *the end,* Matt. xxv. 34, first call Himself by the title of THE KING. The name will no sooner be won, than laid at the feet of the Father, thus completing by the last great act of Redemption, the obedience which He manifested in His Incarnation, and in His death." Alford's observations are excellent. I am somewhat amazed that such a highly respected scholar was not more surely followed on these observations. In other words, Alford observes that Messiah "delivers up the Kingdom to God" at the beginning of His reign, after subduing His enemies, and not at the end of the thousand year reign.

In summary, remember the following facts: (1) the *"end"* in view is the time *"when He* [Messiah] *abolishes all rule and all authority and power"*; (2) this happens in fulfillment of Psalm 110:1, when *"all enemies are made the footstool of His feet"* at the second coming of Christ; (3) having subdued all enemies, including the last one—*"Death,"* which means that this is the time of the resurrection of the Old Testament and Tribulation saints, which is the last phase or "order" in the subjugation of physical Death for God's people; (4) according to Daniel and the prophets, this resurrection is at *"the end"* or *"the last days"* at Messiah's coming; (5) according to the Feast typology outlining God's prophetic time clock, the last Feast is held at *"the end of the year;"* (6) it is at this time of supreme victory over all His enemies that the Messiah *"delivers the Kingdom to God"* and, as the chosen Messiah, He will begin His rule for the next thousand years and (7) the resurrection of the unjust is not in view. That resurrection is at the end of Christ's thousand year reign; furthermore, it is *not* an "*enemy*" and is *not* "*abolished*," but is called "*the Second Death.*"

## "*Deliver*[ing] *the Kingdom to God*" (Verse 24)

What does it mean "*to deliver the Kingdom to God*"? It is important to remember that in the Millennial Kingdom the Messiah (Christ) functions as a Mediatorial King. That is, Christ is the administrator of His Father's Kingdom. Throughout the Gospel accounts the Kingdom is described as "*My Father's Kingdom*," "*the Kingdom of Heaven*," or "*the Kingdom of God* [meaning the Father]." In the book of Daniel, chapter 7 verses 9–14, we are given a preview of what takes place in heaven immediately prior to the second coming of Jesus Christ. "The Son of Man" (one of the titles of Christ) is said to be "brought near to the Ancient of Days [God the Father]" from Whom He receives "*a Kingdom*." This Kingdom is to be set up upon the earth when Christ comes "in the clouds of Heaven." It is a very vivid scene. Christ, therefore, becomes the administrator of His Father's Kingdom to be set up on the earth.

At the spectacular event of the second coming, the Messiah will first rule "*in the midst of His enemies*" according to Psalm 110:2, which we read earlier. He will do battle with all the enemies, conquering and subduing them. The various human, earthly "*rulers, authorities and powers*" will be destroyed or brought into subjugation. The "*last enemy*" to thus be subdued is said to be "*Death,*" itself. This means the subjugation of Death for the final company of the righteous, and this will, therefore, mean their resurrection from the dead at this time. The Kingdom will then be firmly established throughout the earth and the Messiah will stand supreme as "*King of kings and Lord of lords*" (1 Tim. 6:15). In Daniel, the second chapter, verse 35 tells us that after smashing all earthly kingdoms into dust, the Messiah's Kingdom will literally grow and "*fill the earth.*"

It is very appropriate in light of all these facts that the Son of God, in turn, having subdued all enemies, will deliver His authority in direct submission back to the Father Whom He is representing. In other words, "*delivering the Kingdom to God*" is not an act which takes place at the very end of His reign of one thousand years. Rather, it is the grand triumph, in which the Kingdom is firmly established, and will be administered by the Son *in full submission to the Father*. This grand act of submission happens at the very *beginning* of Messiah's reign. It will be the celebration of triumph and the proclamation of the Father's supreme authority.

Again, I will affirm that this "delivering of the Kingdom to God" is not talking about lifting up the Kingdom, as if it were some great package, and transferring it back into His Father's hands in the future new heavens and earth. On the contrary, it is the grand event recognizing the success and victory of the Son of God in establishing God's Kingdom on earth. It is the crowning achievement of destroying God's enemies and establishing the Kingdom in force on earth, and then placing that Kingdom under the headship and authority of God the Father in heaven —

> *. . . then shall the Son also Himself be subject unto Him Who put all things under Him, that God may be All in All.* (1 Cor. 15:28).

Please notice that at the time Messiah sets up the Kingdom, many passages of Scripture record the praise, honor, glory and submission given to the Father (Rev. 5:13; 11:15; 12:10; Matt. 6:9–13; Obad. 21; Dan. 7:27, etc., etc.). The ultimate purpose of all Christ's work is to the exaltation of the Father — Philippians 2:10, 11.

This truth of Christ offering up the Kingdom to God is illustrated for us in the Bible by the account of King David having subdued most of his enemies, having been given a degree of rest and peace in his domain, and in turn giving all praise and submission to God in heaven (read 2 Sam. 7:1 and verses 18–29). David cried out at that beautiful moment, as he contemplated building a house for God,

> *Let Thy Name be magnified forever, saying, the Lord of Hosts is the God over Israel: and let the house of Thy servant David be established before Thee.*

In other words, David was recognizing that the kingdom belonged to God and that His name alone should be praised. David was a mediatorial king ruling under the direct leadership and headship of God, a theocracy on earth. Thus, David's kingdom was actually called "The Kingdom of the Lord over Israel" and "The Kingdom of the Lord in the hands of the sons of David" (see 1 Chron. 28:5 and 2 Chron. 13:8).

This truth is repeated again at the time Solomon was about to assume the Kingdom (see 1 Chron. 29:10–13). The exact words of David in praise to God were,

> *Thine, O Lord, is the GREATNESS, and the POWER, and the GLORY, and the VICTORY, and the MAJESTY: for all that is in heaven and in the earth is Thine; THINE IS THE KINGDOM, O LORD, and Thou art exalted as HEAD ABOVE ALL.*

This is precisely what Jesus Christ, the Mediatorial King, will say and do at the time of His coronation and triumph (see Matt. 6:10–13). This is what it means to *"offer the Kingdom to the Father."* The Messiah (Anointed Prince) will have triumphed and will be placing Himself and the Kingdom under the authority of God the Father in heaven.

### *"For He has put all things in subjection under His feet"* (Verses 27 and 28)

In verses 27 and 28 the apostle Paul quoted from a second passage to affirm the same basic truth of Christ's victory and accomplishments and then the ultimate submission of all to God the Father. This quotation is from Psalm 8 and verse 6. It is similar in nature to Psalm 110:1 as it would apply to Jesus Christ. However, when one looks at Psalm 8, it is first of all evident that it is speaking about the place of rule which God has given to Adam and to his posterity. Nevertheless, there is a double application of this Psalm. Since Christ is also referred to as "the Second Man" and "the Last Adam" (see 1 Cor. 15:45–47), and since *"Adam is a figure of Him*

*Who was to come*" (Rom. 5:14), it is perfectly appropriate to apply the truth of this Psalm to "the Second Man," as well. That is what Paul is doing in 1 Corinthians 15:27 and 28.

It is interesting to note that Paul quoted from these same two Psalms in the book of Hebrews as well as here in 1 Corinthians 15. In Hebrews 1:13 Paul quoted from Psalm 110:1 and applied it directly to Christ. Then, in very close proximity, in Hebrews 2:5–9 he quoted from Psalm 8:4–6 and also applied this to Christ in a secondary manner, saying, "*We do not yet see all things put under Him. But we see Jesus, . . .*" (vs. 8 and 9). This is the same thing Paul was doing in 1 Corinthians 15, with the exception of the "*not yet all things.*"

In the passage before us in 1 Corinthians 15, Paul made it clear that it is God's intent to subject all things to Christ. The "*all things*" in 1 Corinthians 15 are specified as "*all* [earthly] *rule, authority and power.*" This has to do with the physical sphere in which He is going to set up the Kingdom of God on earth. *"When"* that event happens, at the second coming of Christ to subdue all His enemies including "Death," *"then"* the Son, Himself, will be subjected to God the Father, that God may be *"All in All."*

### A Summary Application

### (1) 1 Corinthians 15:20–26
*But now Christ has been raised from the dead,
    the first fruits of those who are asleep.*
For since by a man came death, by a Man also
    came the resurrection of the dead.
For as in Adam all die, so also in Christ all will
    be made alive!
But each in his own order [rank or class]:
    [1] *Christ the first fruits,*
    [2] after that those who are Christ's at His coming,
    [3] then the end, [when] . . . the last enemy that will be
    abolished is death.

## (2) 1 Thessalonians 4:14–17

For if we believe that Jesus died and rose again,
even so God will bring with Him [in resurrection]
those who have fallen asleep in Jesus.
For this we say to you by the word of the Lord,
that we who are alive and remain until the coming
of the Lord will not precede those who have
fallen asleep.
For the Lord Himself will descend from heaven with
a shout, with the voice of an archangel and with
the trumpet of God, and *the dead in Christ* will
rise first. *Then we who are alive and remain will be
caught up together with them in the clouds to meet
the Lord in the air.* And thus we shall always be
with the Lord.

## (3) Job 19:25–27 (NASB)

As for me, I know that my Redeemer lives,
and at the last [Lit., *in the end*] *He will take His
stand on the earth.*
*Even after my skin is destroyed, yet in my flesh
I shall see God; Whom I myself shall behold,
and my eyes will see and not another.*

Note the distinctions and the contrasts between number (2) and
(3). In (2), the Rapture, the resurrected are "caught up . . . in the
clouds" to meet Christ "*in the air*." Whereas, in (3), they will meet
Messiah "*on the earth.*" In (2) living saints are translated with the
resurrected dead as well. In (3) there is no translation of the living
saints. In (2) there is the Rapture, a snatching away, or being "caught
up." In (3) this is simply not the case.

### A Summary Statement

If I were to summarize this Bible study in an abbreviated manner,
I would do so by the following outline statement concerning—

## *The Threefold Order*
## *of the Resurrection of the Righteous*

*First*, the Wave Offering of the Firstfruits
at the Feast of Unleavend Bread
symbolizing the resurrection and ascension of Christ—
the "Firstfruits" of the dead—in resurrection.

*Second*, the Wave Offering of the two Loaves of Bread
at the Feast of Pentecost
symbolizing the resurrection and ascension of the Church—
the Firstfruits Harvest—"They that are Christ's."

*Third*, the final Ingathering of Harvest at the End of the year,
at the Feast of Tabernacles
symbolizing the resurrection of Old Testament and Tribulation
Saints—the final Harvest at "the end," in which
"Death is abolished."

*Chapter Eight*

# A SECONDARY APPLICATION

### *A Secondary Spiritual Application*

There is a secondary application concerning this truth about God having "all things put under His [Christ's] feet" (Ps. 8:6) which is fulfilled in a vital spiritual sense for this present Church Age. Though it is clear here in 1 Corinthians 15 that the apostle Paul applied the principle of Psalm 8:6 to the beginning of Christ's future reign, yet it is also true that Paul made another application of Psalm 8:6 to Christ's victorious work in defeating Satan in His death, burial and resurrection at the beginning of *the present Age*. In fact, the victorious work of Christ in obtaining redemption for mankind is so pronounced in the theology of Paul's epistles that we could just as well say that this spiritual reality is the "primary application" of Psalm 8 which Paul made. In this case, the "secondary application" would actually be the future application to His accomplishments at the second coming of Christ in the beginning of His Millennial Reign.

In 1 John 3:8 we are told, "For this purpose the Son of God was manifested, *that He might destroy the works of the Devil.*" In 2 Timothy 1:10 we are given those glorious words about "the appearing of our Savior Jesus Christ, Who has *abolished Death* and *brought life and immortality to light through the gospel.*" In Colossians 2:10–15 we are informed that the believer is "complete in Him, *Who is the head of all principality and power.*" And "He has forgiven us all trespasses, having wiped out the handwriting of requirements that was against us, which was contrary to us. And He has taken it out of the way, having nailed it to the cross, *having disarmed principalities and powers, He made a public spectacle of them, triumphing over them in it.*" Once again, in Ephesians 1:20–23 Paul was inspired to say of God's work for us in Christ ". . . which He brought about in Christ *when He raised Him from the dead, and seated Him at His right hand in the heavenly places, far above all rule and authority and power and dominion, and every name that is named, not only in this Age, but also in the Age to come. And 'He put all things in subjection under His feet'* [Ps. 8:6], *and gave Him as Head over all things to the Church which is His body, the fullness of Him Who fills* **all in all**."

It is clear that this is the vital *spiritual* work of Christ in victory over the spiritual authorities and powers on our behalf. The apostle Peter (1 Pet. 3:22) added, concerning Christ, "*Who is at the right hand of God, having gone into heaven, after angels and authorities and powers had been subjected to Him.*" The subjection of the spiritual forces as a result of Christ's victory in His death, burial and resurrection is paramount to Christ's future *physical* victory over the satanically inspired national forces on earth which will be accomplished at His second coming.

The application of Psalm 8:6 to the victorious work Christ accomplished over Satan in His substitutionary death, burial and resurrection is absolutely necessary in order for the application of this principle to the actual future physical reign on earth. The important difference between these two applications is that one concerns itself with Christ's *spiritual* defeat of Satan as He provided *spiritual* redemption for mankind, whereas the other concerns itself with Christ's defeat of Satan in the *physical* realm of Satan's control over the nations. First of all, Christ must have defeated Satan in the *spiritual* realm of his spiritual control over the souls of men because of sin. Obviously, redemption from the guilt and penalty of sin is a necessary prerequisite to Christ ruling over mankind on a redeemed earth. Only after the spiritual victory could He ever defeat Satan in the *physical* realm of his control over the physical kingdoms on earth.

These two different applications concerning the "abolishment of death" and the placing of "all things under Christ's feet" can easily be confused unless we see and accept both applications. Sad to say, once again, many teachers in Christendom will quote one application to cancel out or to misinterpret the application of the other. However, each are true in its own sphere. Man is not merely a fleshly body; he is primarily a spiritual entity dwelling in a physical body. Death is not merely a physical phenomenon; it is first of all spiritual separation from the life that is in and with God. We must first of all obtain "everlasting *spiritual* life" before we could ever be granted the blessing of "everlasting *physical* life." There must be the abolishment of death *spiritually* before there can be the abolishment of death *physically*. Thus "death is abolished" in two different stages.

In Christ's substitutionary death for the sins of all mankind of all the ages, He has taken "the sting" out of death (1 Cor. 15:56). Christ paid the death penalty! Therefore, there is no longer the fear of death for those who trust in Christ. The essential death which separated man and God is abolished. Believers are recreated in Christ as "new creatures" (2 Cor. 5:17). The life and fellowship with God has been restored. In addition, Christ, in His glorious resurrection from the dead, gives all believers the "guarantee" of our future resurrections from physical death, as well. This is when "death will be abolished" as to the physical bodily resurrection from death and/ or the glorification of those saints who have not died physically.

## The Unfolding of These Two Applications

I would like to explain further why there are these two distinctive applications of this principle and how they are unfolding in time by the following manner—

When the Son of God came to earth, He came as "a Minister to *the Circumcision* for the truth of God, to confirm *the promises* made to *the fathers*" (Rom. 15:8). They were promised a literal, earthly kingdom, wherein they would be delivered from all their enemies, and so it is stated in Luke 1:68–72,

> Blessed be the Lord God of Israel, for He has visited
> and redeemed *His people*, and has raised up a horn
> of salvation for us in the house of His servant *David,*
> as He spoke by the mouth of His *holy prophets*, who
> have been since the world began, that we should be
> saved from our *enemies* and from the hand of all who
> hate us, to perform the mercy *promised to our fathers*
> and to remember His holy covenant.

Therefore, Christ was literally born as a direct descendent of King David, for the Messiah Who would reign must be a descendent of David (Rom.1:3). Many other things Christ did, too numerous to even list here, which were fulfilled literally and physically in preparation for that prophesied Kingdom.

However, as we all well know, Israel rejected her Messiah, and the Kingdom, which was offered to her, was taken away to be given to another generation (Matt. 21:43). (Please see the Bible study on my web site, *The Kingdom of God*, which explains this more fully.) The establishment of this Millennial Kingdom was postponed by reason of Israel's national rejection of her King.

The enemies of Christ would propagandize this as an evidence of failure and Christ as being a false Messiah. It would thus seem to many that the prophesies of John the Baptist, Christ and the disciples that *"the Kingdom of God was nigh at hand"* (Mark 1:14, 15) would fall to the ground in failure. But God did not deem it proper to allow their voices to thus appear to be false. Therefore, in God's predetermined plan there was, indeed, a Kingdom which was set up. This came as a result of Christ's sin-conquering death, burial and glorious resurrection from the dead, with the keys of Death and Hell. However, it was not the prophesied Messianic kingdom; it was rather a spiritual phase of the Kingdom to be established instead. Indeed, towards the end of Christ's ministry, He spoke of a spiritual aspect of the Kingdom of God (John 18:36 and Luke 17:20, 21). This Kingdom would apply to the present Church Age (Rom. 14:17 and Col. 1:13). This present spiritual Age is parenthetical in nature until such time as the prophesied physical Kingdom should be established. So, therefore, Bible readers must distinguish between the literal, earthly, Messianic Kingdom and the present, spiritual Kingdom of God.

Another illustration of this principle is in the prophecies about a coming "baptism of the Holy Spirit" made by John the Baptist (Matt. 3:11, etc.). John was actually not talking about the baptism of the Holy Spirit which characterizes this particular Age, because this Age was a "mystery" which was not made known in past times (Eph. 3:1–7). John the Baptist was talking about the outpouring of the Holy Spirit which the prophets spoke of, which would happen at the beginning of Messiah's Millennial reign (Isa. 32:15; 44:3; Ezek. 36:25–33; Joel 2:28, etc.). However, in light of Israel's rejection of Christ and the postponement of that Kingdom, it is again true that God would not allow John's words to fall to the ground as if unfulfilled. In God's plan, a baptism of the Holy Spirit did take place, but not the one prophesied in the Hebrew Scriptures. Christ told the disciples privately about *"the promise of the Father"* the night of His betrayal (John 14, 15 and 16). This baptism is absolutely unique for this Church Age, "for by one Spirit are we all baptized into one body" (1 Cor. 12:13). This characterizes the present, spiritual Kingdom of God.

We can illustrate this principle of double or multiple application again by the prophecy of Christ now being the "chief cornerstone" (Acts 4:11; Eph. 2:20 and 1 Pet. 2:6 and 7) for His Church. However, in their original settings, the prophesies of Messiah as the "chief cornerstone" apply to Christ in the Kingdom Age and pertain to His rule on earth over Israel (Psalm 118:22–26 and Isa. 28:16). This is when the rejected Messiah will indeed reign over a repentant Israel. Therefore, this prophecy is applied to the present Church Age in a secondary manner only.

### Spiritual Application Today

Thus it is, just before the beginning of this present spiritual Kingdom, Christ, in His death, burial and resurrection, is said to have "conquered him who had the power of death, that is, the Devil" (Heb. 2:14). Likewise, as I gave before, there is an abundance of references made by Paul and the other apostles which speak of the many accomplishments of Christ in His sin-conquering death, His descent into Hell and His glorious resurrection from Hell with the very keys of Death and Hell. Therefore, it can be understood that when Christ ascended on high and sat down at the right hand of the Father, He subjected Himself to the Father in preparation for the coming spiritual phase of the Kingdom of God. Consequently, it is realistic to understand that after the resurrection of Christ into His glory, having subdued Satan in the spiritual realm and guaranteed spiritual life and a future physical resurrection for all believers, He delivered up the spiritual Kingdom to the Father, and sat down at His Father's right hand so that God the Father might be "all in all."

One of the unique characteristics of this present spiritual Kingdom (Rom. 14:17 and Col. 1:13) is the fact that, positionally, of all believers it is said ". . . Who blessed us with every *spiritual blessing* in *the heavenly places in Christ*" (Eph. 1:3, 19–23).

That there was a tremendous spiritual warfare going on at the time of Christ's crucifixion, and in His bearing away our sins under the judgment of God, becomes very clear in the teachings of the Spirit of God through the apostles. By taking upon Himself all our sins, Christ humiliated Satan and his forces of evil and gave eternal life unto all who trust in Him. The supreme significance of this achievement meant that all spiritual authorities had become subjected to Christ. That accomplished victory has paved the way for the future victory over Satan in the physical realm of his rulership on earth.

Please take note of, and study carefully the accompanying charts on this important subject. The accomplishments of Christ at His death and resurrection should never be confused with those accomplishments yet to come at His second advent. These charts are entitled *The Crowning Victory and Exaltation of Christ—No. 1, Spiritual* and *No. 2, Physical*. In between these two is the chart on the additional theme of victory at the *Rapture* of the Church.

## Conclusion

I am indeed thankful for the ministry of Maurice M. Johnson in his emphasis upon this great victory which Christ accomplished by His death and resurrection. Furthermore, we should not allow the distinctive truths of each of these two different Kingdoms to cancel out each other in our minds. These are apparently contradictory entities *unless* we separate the two spheres of victory and defeat of Satan—one, spiritual and one, physical. In biblical carefulness, we must not allow the beautiful truths of the spiritual application to block out the spectacular application to the events surrounding the second coming of Christ which many teachers attempt to do.

## Please Take Note of the Following Charts

1. Israel's Sacred Year Calendar

2. "The Appointed Times of the Lord"

3. The Threefold Order of the Resurrection of the Righteous

4. The Future "Week" of Prophecy

5. The Crowning Victory and Exaltation of Christ,
   # 1, Spiritual

6. Subduing Death in Victory at the Rapture, (Parenthetical)

7. The Crowning Victory and Exaltation of Christ,
   # 2, Physical

8. Satan's Subjugation in Three Successive Stages

# Chart 1. Israel's Sacred Year Calendar

**ISRAEL'S SACRED YEAR CALENDAR**
"The [7 •] Appointed Times of the LORD" (Heb., *mo'adim*)
"The [3] Feasts" (Heb., *haggim*, or *chag*), (also Civil Holidays added later)

| Months | | 3 Pilgrimage Fesivals & Holydays | | | High |
| Current Hebrew Name | Roman Gregorian | Name of Day or Feast | Hebrew Name | Day of Month | Sab-bath* |
|---|---|---|---|---|---|
| Regular 7th day Sabbaths are listed as Holy Convocations, Lev. 23:3 | | | | | |
| 1. Nisan | March – | (Passover Selected) | | 10th | |
| or Abib | April | Passover Sacrificed | *Pesah* | 14th | |
| | | 1. Feast of Unleavened Bread | *Pesah* or *Matzah* | 15th– 21st | * 1 * 2 |
| | | Firstfruit Offering made during Feast– Sun. | | | |
| 2. Iyyar or Ziv | April – May | | | | |
| 3. Sivan | May – | 2. Feast of Weeks | *Shavuot* | 50th | * 3 |
| | June | (or Pentecost – New Meal Offering) | | | |
| 4. Tammuz | June – July | | | | |
| 5. Ab or Av | July – Aug. | Fast for the Destruction of the Temple by Nebuchadnezzar | | 9th | |
| 6. Elul | Aug. – Sept. | | | | |
| The New Year on Israel's Civil Calendar begins on 1st of Tishri, Called *Rosh Hashanah* (the New Year), (tradition supposedly from Neh. 8:1–12). | | | | | |
| 7. Tishri or Ethanim | Sept. – Oct. | Trumpets | *Shofar* | 1st | * 4 |
| | | Day of Atonement | *Yom Kippur* | 10th | * 5 |
| | | 3. Feast of Tabernacles or Ingathering | *Sukkat* | 15th – 22nd | * 6 * 7 |
| 8. Heshvan | Oct. – Nov. | | | | |
| 9. Kislev or Chislev | Nov. – Dec. | Dedication or Lights | *Hanukkah* | 25th | |
| 10. Tevet | Dec. – Jan. | | | | |
| 11. Shevat | Jan. – Feb. | | | | |
| 12. Adar | Feb. – March | Lots | *Purim* | 14th – 15th | |

## Chart 2. "The Appointed Times of the Lord"

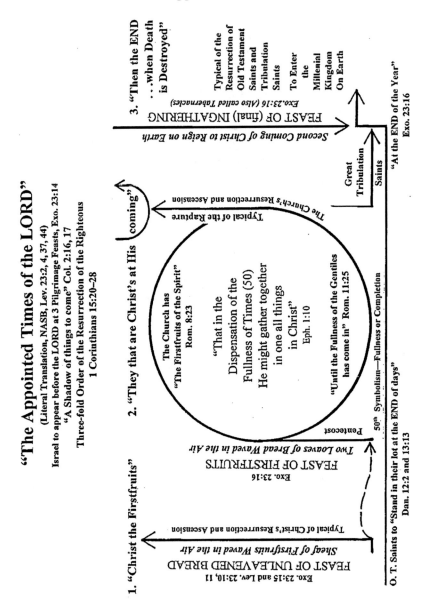

# Chart 3  The Threefold Order of the Resurrection of the Righteous

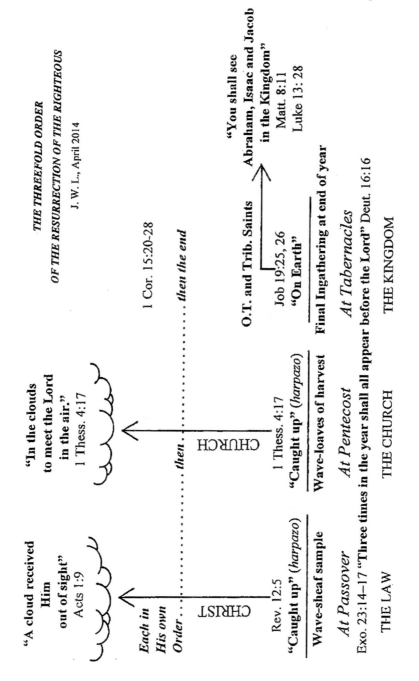

**THE THREEFOLD ORDER**
*OF THE RESURRECTION OF THE RIGHTEOUS*

J. W. L., April 2014

"A cloud received Him out of sight"
Acts 1:9

"In the clouds to meet the Lord in the air."
1 Thess. 4:17

"You shall see Abraham, Isaac and Jacob in the Kingdom"
Matt. 8:11
Luke 13: 28

1 Cor. 15:20-28

. . . . . *then the end*

CHRIST

CHURCH

O.T. and Trib. Saints

Job 19:25, 26
"On Earth"

*Each in His own Order* . . . . .

. . . *then* . . .

Rev. 12:5
"Caught up" (*harpazo*)

1 Thess. 4:17
"Caught up" (*harpazo*)

Wave-sheaf sample

Wave-loaves of harvest

Final Ingathering at end of year

*At Passover*

*At Pentecost*

*At Tabernacles*

Exo. 23:14–17 "Three times in the year shall all appear before the Lord" Deut. 16:16

THE LAW

THE CHURCH

THE KINGDOM

## Chart 4. The Future "Week" of Prophecy (a)

# THE FUTURE "WEEK" OF PROPHECY ACCORDING TO DANIEL & REVELATION

| |  |
|---|---|
| 1. | "COVENANT FOR ONE WEEK - 7 YEARS" — DAN.9:27 |
| 2. | "SACRIFICE TO CEASE IN MIDST OF WEEK" — DAN.9:27 |
| 3. | "OPPRESSION OF SAINTS" / "Times, Time & 1/2 Time" — DAN.7:25 |
| 4. | "HOLY PEOPLE SCATTERED" / "Times, Time & 1/2 Time" — DAN.12:7 |
| 5. | "ISRAEL NOURISHED" / "Times, Time & 1/2 Time" — REV.12:14 |
| 6. | "TEMPLE GIVE TO GENTILES" / "42 Months" — REV.11:2 |

"CLEANSED," DANIEL 8:14

1. The future "week of prophecy is a week of years determined upon the nation Israel. [All expressions regarding time periods are based on Hebrew reckoning. They had a lunar calendar with 12 months per year, 30 days per month, equaling 360 days per year. Once every several years they would insert an extra month in order to accommodate the extra days accumulated each year.]

2. The "midst of the week" becomes the dividing line for the last 3 1/2 years of time called "the Great Tribulation."

3., 4., 5. "Time" (singular) equals one year. "Times" (plural) equals two years. "Dividing of Time" equals 1/2 year.

6. & 7. The "42 months" are simply 12 months per year times 3 1/2 yrs. = 42.

## Chart 4. The Future "Week" of Prophecy (b)

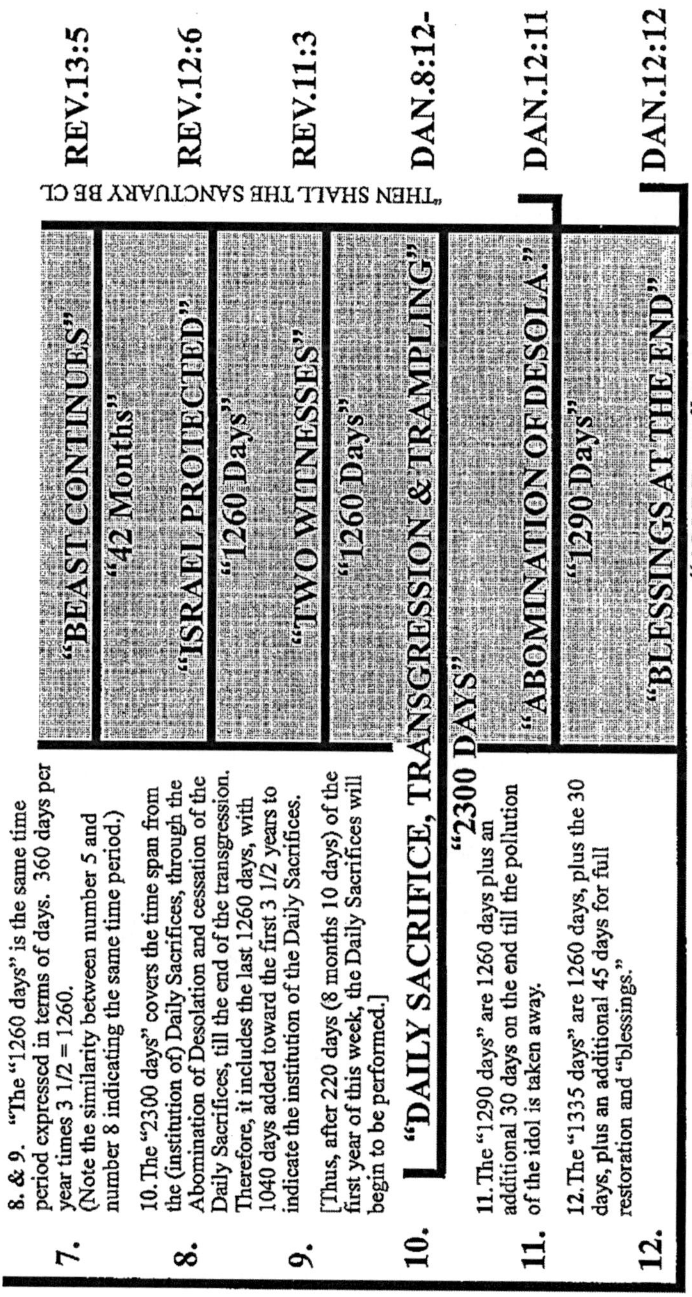

REV.13:5  REV.12:6  REV.11:3  DAN.8:12-  DAN.12:11  DAN.12:12

"THEN SHALL THE SANCTUARY BE CL."

"BEAST CONTINUES"

"42 Months"

"ISRAEL PROTECTED"

"1260 Days"

"TWO WITNESSES"

"1260 Days"

"DAILY SACRIFICE, TRANSGRESSION & TRAMPLING"

"2300 DAYS"

"ABOMINATION OF DESOLA."

"1290 Days"

"BLESSINGS AT THE END"

"1335 Days"

**7.** 8. & 9. "The "1260 days" is the same time period expressed in terms of days. 360 days per year times 3 1/2 = 1260. [Note the similarity between number 5 and number 8 indicating the same time period.]

**8.** The "2300 days" covers the time span from the (institution of) Daily Sacrifices, through the Abomination of Desolation and cessation of the Daily Sacrifices, till the end of the transgression. Therefore, it includes the last 1260 days, with 1040 days added toward the first 3 1/2 years to indicate the institution of the Daily Sacrifices.

**9.** [Thus, after 220 days (8 months 10 days) of the first year of this week, the Daily Sacrifices will begin to be performed.]

**10.** "DAILY SACRIFICE, TRANSGRESSION & TRAMPLING" "2300 DAYS"

**11.** The "1290 days" are 1260 days plus an additional 30 days on the end till the pollution of the idol is taken away.

**12.** The "1335 days" are 1260 days, plus the 30 days, plus an additional 45 days for full restoration and "blessings."

## Chart 5. The Crowning Victory and Exaltation of Christ, # 1, Spiritual (a)

**Eph. 1:19-23**
"And what is the exceeding greatness of His power to usward who believe, according to the working of His mighty power, which He wrought in Christ, when He raised Him from the dead, and set Him at His own right hand in the heavenly places, far above all principality, and power, and might, and dominion, and every name that is named, not only in this age, but also in that which is to come: and hath put all things under His feet, and gave Him to be head over all things to the church, which is His body, the fulness of Him that filleth all in all."

**Philip. 2:10**
"That at the name of Jesus every knee should bow, of the things in heaven, and things in earth, and things under the earth."

**Acts 2:33**
"Therefore being by the right hand of God, exalted."
(See also--Heb.1:3; 8:1; & 12:2).

**I Pet. 3:22**
"Who has gone into heaven and is on the right hand of God; angels and authorities and powers being made subject unto Him."

**Col. 2:15**
"And having spoiled principalities and powers, He made a shew of them openly, triumphing over them in it."

**Col. 2:10**
"And ye are complete in Him, which is the head of all principality and power."

**Matt. 28:18**
"And Jesus said... All power is given unto Me in heaven and in earth,"

**John 16:11**
"The prince of this world is judged."

# THE CROWNING VICTORY AND EXALTATION OF CHRIST
## At His First Coming

## No. I, Spiritual

**Philip. 2:5-7**
"Let this mind be in you, which was also in Christ Jesus: Who, being in the form of God, thought it not robbery to be equal with God: but made Himself of no reputation, and took upon Him the form of a servant, and was made in the likeness of men:"

98

## Chart 5.  The Crowning Victory and Exaltation of Christ, # 1, Spiritual (b)

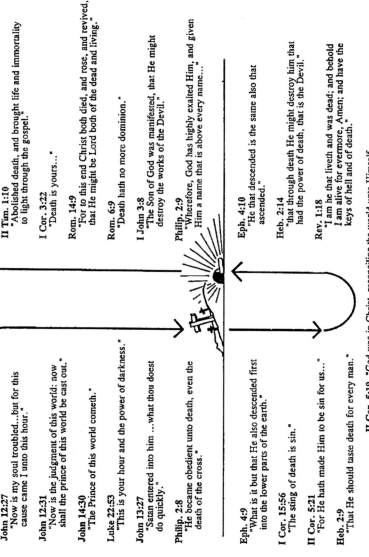

II Tim. 1:10
"Abolished death, and brought life and immorality to light through the gospel."

I Cor. 3:22
"Death is yours..."

Rom. 14:9
"For to this end Christ both died, and rose, and revived, that He might be Lord both of the dead and living."

Rom. 6:9
"Death hath no more dominion."

I John 3:8
"The Son of God was manifested, that He might destroy the works of the Devil."

Philip. 2:9
"Wherefore, God has highly exalted Him, and given Him a name that is above every name..."

Eph. 4:10
"He that descended is the same also that ascended."

Heb. 2:14
"that through death He might destroy him that had the power of death, that is the Devil."

Rev. 1:18
"I am he that liveth and was dead; and behold I am alive for evermore, Amen; and have the keys of hell and of death."

John 12:27
"Now is my soul troubled....but for this cause came I unto this hour."

John 12:31
"Now is the judgment of this world: now shall the prince of this world be cast out."

John 14:30
"The Prince of this world cometh."

Luke 22:53
"This is your hour and the power of darkness."

John 13:27
"Satan entered into him ...what thou doest do quickly."

Philip. 2:8
"He became obedient unto death, even the death of the cross."

Eph. 4:9
"What is it but that He also descended first into the lower parts of the earth."

I Cor. 15:56
"The sting of death is sin."

II Cor. 5:21
"For He hath made Him to be sin for us..."

Heb. 2:9
"That He should taste death for every man."

II Cor. 5:19  "God was in Christ, reconciling the world unto Himself, not imputing their trespasses unto them."

## Chart 6. Subduing Death in Victory at the Rapture, (Parenthetical) (a)

By J.W.L. 1990

## SUBDUING DEATH IN VICTORY

## AT THE RAPTURE (Parenthetical)

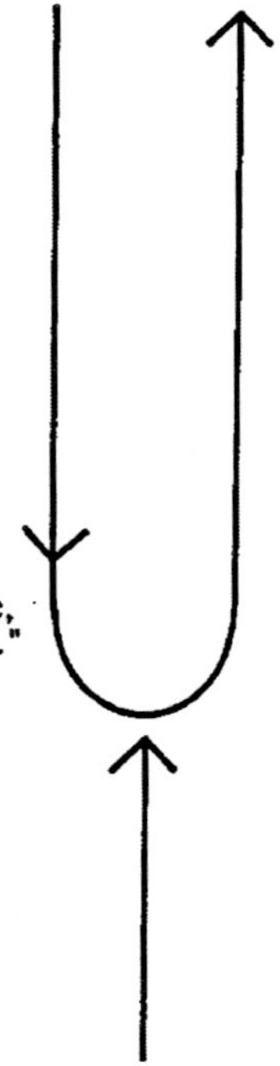

**I Thess. 4:13-18**
"...And the dead in Christ shall rise first: then we which are alive and remain shall be caught up together with them in the clouds to meet the Lord in the air: and so shall we ever be with the Lord. Wherefore, COMFORT one another with these words."

**Philip. 3:20**
"For our conversation is in heaven; from whence also we look for the Saviour, the Lord Jesus Christ: Who shall change our vile body, that it may be fashioned like unto His glorious body, according to the working whereby He is able even to SUBDUE ALL THINGS unto Himself."

**John 14:2,3**
"In My Father's house are many mansions: if it were not so I would have told you. I go to prepare a place for you. And if I go and prepare a place for you, I will come again, and receive you unto Myself; that where I am, there ye may be also."

**Col. 1:27**
"To whom God would make known what is the riches of the Glory of this Mystery among the Gentiles; which is Christ in you, the Hope of Glory."

**Titus 2:13**
"Looking for that Blessed Hope, and the glorious appearing of the great God and our Saviour Jesus Christ."

## Chart 6. Subduing Death in Victory at the Rapture, (Parenthetical) (b)

**Rom. 8:11**
"But if the Spirit of Him that raised up Jesus from the dead dwell in you, He that raised up Christ from the dead shall also quicken your mortal bodies by His Spirit that dwelleth in you."

**Rom. 8:18-23**
"For I reckon that the sufferings of this present time are not worthy to be compared with the glory which shall be revealed in us. For the earnest expectation of the creation waiteth for the manifestation of the sons of God...because the creation itself also shall be delivered from the bondage of corruption into the glorious liberty of the children of God. For the whole creation GROANETH and travaileth in pain together until now. And not only they, but ourselves also, which have the firstfruits of the Spirit, even we ourselves GROAN within ourselves, waiting for the adoption, to wit the REDEMPTION of our body..."

**II Tim. 4:8**
"Henceforth there is laid up for me a crown of righteousness, which the Lord, the righteous judge, shall give me at that day: and not to me only, but unto all them that love His appearing."

**I Cor. 15:54**
"Behold, I shew you a mystery; we shall not all sleep, but we shall all be changed, in a moment, in the twinkling of an eye, at the last trump: for the trumpet shall sound, and the dead shall be raised incorruptible, and we shall be changed. For this corruptible shall have put on incorruption, and this mortal must put on immortality, then shall be brought to pass the saying that is written, DEATH IS SWALLOWED UP IN VICTORY. O DEATH, where is thy sting? O grave, where is thy victory?"

**II Cor. 5:2-4**
"For in this we groan, earnestly desiring to be clothed upon with our house which is from heaven: If so that being clothed we shall not be found naked. For we that are in this tabernacle do GROAN, being BURDENED: not for that we would be unclothed, but clothed upon, that mortality might be SWALLOWED up of LIFE."

**Eph. 1:13,14**
"In whom also after that ye believed, ye were sealed with that Holy Spirit of promise, which is the earnest of our inheritance until the Redemption of the purchased posession, unto the praise of His glory."

## Chart 7. The Crowning Victory and Exaltation of Christ, # 2, Physical (a)

# THE CROWNING VICTORY AND EXALTATION OF CHRIST At His Second Coming

# No. II, Physical

**Acts 3:21**
"Whom the heaven must receive until the time of restitution of all things, which God hath spoken by the mouth of all His holy prophets since the world began."

**Dan. 7:13,14**
"And I saw...and behold, one like the Son of Man came with the clouds of heaven, and came to the Ancient of Days, and they brought Him near before Him. And there was given to Him Dominion, and Glory, and a Kingdom, that all people, nations, and languages, should serve Him: His DOMINION is an everlasting DOMINION."

**II Pet. 1:16,17**
"For we have not followed cunningly devised fables, when we made known unto you the Power and Coming of our Lord Jesus Christ, but were eyewitnesses of His Majesty. For He received from God the Father HONOR and GLORY.",

**Matt. 26:64**
"Hereafter shall ye see the Son of Man sitting on the right hand of Power, and coming in the clouds of heaven."

**Matt. 24:30**
"And then shall appear the sign of the Son of Man in heaven: and then shall all the tribes of the earth mourn, and they shall see the Son of Man coming in the clouds of heaven with Power and Great Glory."

**Rev. 6:15, 16**
"And the kings of the earth, and the great men, and the rich men, and the chief captains, and the mighty men, and every bondman, and every free man, hid themselves in the dens and in the rocks of the mountains...hide us from the face of Him that sitteth upon the throne, and from the Wrath of the Lamb."

**Rev. 2:26,27**
"And he that overcometh, and keepeth My works unto the end, to him will I give power over the nations; and he shall rule them with a rod of iron; as the vessels of a potter shall they be broken to shivers: even as I have received of My Father."

**Heb. 2:5**
"For unto the angels hath He not put in Subjection the world to come, whereof we speak...."

**Zech. 6:12,13; 9:10; 14:9**
"And He shall bear the GLORY, and shall sit and RULE upon His throne...and His DOMINION shall be from sea to sea...even to the ends of the earth...and the Lord shall be KING over ALL the earth"

**I Tim. 6:15**
"Which in His times He shall shew, Who is that blessed and Only Potentate, the King of kings, and Lord of lords."

102

# Chart 7. The Crowning Victory and Exaltation of Christ, # 2, Physical (b)

**Isa. 25:8**
"He will swallow up death in VICTORY; and the Lord God shall wipe away tears..."

**Hosea 13:14**
"I will ransom them from the power of the grave; I will redeem them from death: O death, I will be thy plagues, O grave, I will be thy DESTRUCTION."

**Isa. 26:19**
"Thy dead men shall live, together with my dead body shall they arise. Awake and Sing, ye that dwell in the dust...for the earth shall CAST OUT THE DEAD."

**Isa. 25:7**
"And He will DESTROY in this mountain the face of the covering cast over all people, and the veil that is spread over the nations."

**Rev. 19:15,16**
"And out of His mouth goeth a sharp sword, that with it He shall smite the nations; and He shall rule them with a rod of iron... KING OF KINGS and LORD OF LORDS."

**Psalm 2:6,8**
"Yet have I set My King upon My holy hill of Zion... I shall give Thee the heathen for Thine inheritance, and the uttermost parts of the earth for Thy posession."

**Rev. 11:15-18**
"The kingdoms of this world are become the Kingdoms of our Lord, and of His Christ; and He shall REIGN...and shall DESTROY them that destroy the earth."

**II Thess. 1:9**
"Who shall be punished with everlasting destruction from the presence of the Lord, from the Glory of His Power."

**II Thess. 2:8**
"...that wicked (one) whom the Lord shall consume with the spirit of His mouth, and shall destroy with the brightness of His coming."

**Dan. 2:34,35**
"A Stone was cut out of the mountain without hands, which smote the image upon his feet, then was the Iron, the Clay, the Brass, the Silver, and the Gold, broken to pieces together, and became like the chaff of the summer threshing floor; and the wind carried them away...and the Stone became a great Mountain; and filled all the earth."

**Psalm 110:1,2,3**
"The LORD said to my Lord, sit Thou at My right hand, until I make Thine enemies Thy footstool. The Lord shall send the rod of Thy strength out of Zion: rule Thou in the midst of Thine enemies. Thy people shall be willing in the day of Thy POWER."

**Isa. 42:13**
"The Lord shall go forth as a mighty man, He shall stir up jealousy like a man of war; He shall cry, yea, roar; He shall prevail against His ENEMIES."

**Isa. 24:21-23**
"And it shall come to pass in that day that the Lord shall punish the host of the high ones that are on high, and the kings of the earth upon earth. And they shall be gathered together, as prisoners are gathered in the pit, and shall be shut up in the prison...when the Lord of hosts shall reign in Mount Zion, and in Jerusalem, and before His ancients GLORIOUSLY."

Chart 8. Satan's Subjugation in Three Successive Stages

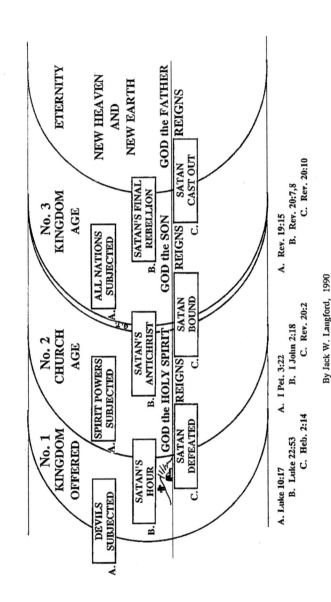

# APPENDIX

Anumber of years after I had seen the parallel between the Harvest Feasts of Israel and the "orders" of the resurrection of the righteous, my attention was directed to a book by the very popular Hal Lindsey entitled *The Rapture*. Towards the conclusion of his book (page 160) he made the observation that "Israel's harvest could be a type of the various stages of the first resurrection." However, his explanations were not positive. At first he left the thought that "stage three will be at the end of the millennium" (page 158). Nevertheless, on page 161 he diagramed this suggestion by a chart of the three stages following the same outline that I have given in this Bible study. The three stages he gave in the following order: Christ the Firstfruits; second, the Church; and third, the Old Testament and Tribulation saints at the second coming of Christ. In this regard, he also stated concerning this view that "these verses seem to indicate that the first resurrection, the one of life, will end with the resurrection of the saints at the end of the tribulation" (page 162). Mr. Lindsey's book was first published in 1982, the same year I had seen the basic principle which I described in the introduction. I was somewhat heartened by this observation because it demonstrated that what I saw was not some whimsical dream; others have seen the possibility of the same basic truth.

In addition, *The Lamplighter*, a publication of "The Lamb & Lion Ministries" by David R. Reagen, has also published a chart depicting this sequence very clearly. It shows the relationship between the three Feasts and the three orders of the resurrection of the righteous. See the March-April 2003 issue and the July-August 2005 issue. I have never seen them make an explanation of this chart.

A few years ago I saw the article by Arnold Fruchtenbaum of the Ariel Ministries. His article was entitled *The Feast of Firstfruits*, Manuscript Number 116, written back in 1985. He saw clearly that there are three orders in the First Resurrection, but he only connected Christ as the "Firstfruits" and did not connect the other "orders" to the other Feasts. On page 6 he stated very clearly, "Not all believers are resurrected at the same time, but in stages. The first stage of the resurrection was Jesus who was the firstfruits of the First Resurrection. But then comes they who are Christ's at His coming. The church saints will be resurrected at the Rapture before the Tribulation. The Old Testament saints and the Tribulation saints will be resurrected after the Second Coming, after the Tribulation."

Above all, are the very clear statements and exposition by the famed Henry Alford in his *New Testament for English Readers*, whom I have made reference to in this study. Though I discovered his thoughts on this subject more recently, yet his works were first published in London between 1849 and 1861. So it is, this truth has actually been understood for a long time.

Even more recently, I have seen the excellent statement made by Jack Kelly on his web site *gracethrufaith.com* in answering the question about "Dating The Rapture." It is well worth repeating here:

> I believe if the Rapture of the Church happens on a Jewish Feast day, then Pentecost would be the most logical one, it being the feast most clearly associated with the Church. But I remain convinced that the Church will be taken on whatever day it reaches its full number based on my understanding of Romans 11:25 and Acts 15:13–18. Since no one knows what the Church's full number is or how close we are to achieving it, I don't believe anyone on Earth will be able to determine the date of our departure in advance.

Brother Jack Kelly may very well appreciate this particular Bible study, in that it harmonizes, on the one hand, the fact that Pentecost is indeed prophetic of the Rapture of the Church and yet, on the other hand, at the very same time it does not make the error of specifying a date, other than designating *"fullness"* as the basic meaning of the number 50. This in turn makes Pentecost in full agreement with— "when the *fullness* of the Gentiles comes in" (Rom. 11:25 and Acts 15:13–18).

# ADDENDOM

## A Positive Demonstration of the Pretribulational Rapture

As an addendum to *The Threefold Order of the Resurrection of the Righteous*, I want to offer what I have used in the past as a simple, but conclusive demonstration of the pretribulational Rapture of the Church of our Lord Jesus Christ. In the previous study it was demonstrated that the Spirit of God led the apostle Paul to clearly distinguish three distinct "orders, ranks or companies" in the resurrection of the righteous. Christ, Himself, was the first "order." The Church of Jesus Christ most certainly composes the second "order." And, all the Old Testament saints and Tribulation martyrs will compose the third and last "order." Now I am going to apply that truth to the popular "debate" in Christendom over the subject of whether or not "the Church which is Christ's body" will go through the prophetic Great Tribulation (Matt. 24:21) which is soon coming upon this Christ-rejecting world.

----

A number of years ago, a Christian friend of mine had come to a place of turmoil in his thinking over the question of the time of the Rapture of the Church. He was beginning to entertain what is called the posttribulational view of the Rapture. This would mean that the

Church would go through the future Great Tribulation time period, spoken of by Christ in Matthew 24:21, and then be "caught up" at Christ's second coming to reign on earth. This brother knew that at one time I had held to that very position. Later, however, some brethren patiently helped me and I became firmly persuaded that I had been wrong on the subject. Thus I came to hold the view which is called "the pretribulational Rapture of the Church." This meant that the Church would be "caught up" to meet Christ at an earlier coming which was exclusively for taking the Church out of this world. So this brother came to me to find out more carefully why I had changed my position. I was pointedly asked by this Christian brother "Can you really prove from the Bible the pretribulational Rapture of the Church?" "Yes," I said, "I believe I can break it down and demonstrate a very simple procedure for any honest person to see!" We went into my study, and there I shared with him some of the following basic Scriptural facts—

### *What is the "Rapture"?*

First, one wants to make sure to establish from the Scriptures exactly what the "Rapture" of the Church is. This is necessary because a lot of people don't even know what it is, or else have very confusing misconceptions about it. Some have even gone so far as to argue that the "Rapture" is a word and doctrine which men have invented and is actually not to be found in the Bible.

Now it is true that the English word "rapture" is not found in our modern English translations of the Bible. However, it is a fact that the word is in the Bible, if one was using the Latin translation. The word "rapture" is simply the anglicized form of the Latin word *raptus* or *rapere*. It just so happens that the oldest and most widespread translation of the Bible up until about A.D. 1700 is the Latin Vulgate, which is still the official translation for the Roman Catholic Church worldwide. So this word has been in the Latin translations of 1 Thessalonians 4:17 from about the second or third century of the present era. In addition, it is not true that the Rapture doctrine is an invention of men. In fact, most scholars today recognize that in all probability the very first book written in the cannon of the

Greek Scriptures is the first letter of Paul to the Thessalonians. We find therein the first mention of the Rapture of the Church. Without quoting all the context, 1 Thessalonians 4:16 and 17 says —

> For the Lord Himself will descend from heaven with a shout, with the voice of an archangel, and with the trumpet of God. And the dead in Christ will rise first. Then we who are alive and remain shall be **caught up together** [*raptiermur,* Latin] with them in the clouds to meet the Lord in the air. And thus we shall always be with the Lord.

Now the words *"caught up"* are from the Greek word *harpazo,* which means "to snatch or catch away" (Strong, # 726). Of this word W. E. Vine says, "This verb conveys the idea of force suddenly exerted." The Latin word *raptus* or *rapere* means the very same thing. It is further helpful to note how this word is used elsewhere in the New Testament. This will demonstrate its meaning beyond any question. In *Vine's Expository Dictionary of New Testament Words,* he lists the following passages which I will quote from the NKJV. I will italicize and underline each time the word *harpazo* is used —

| | |
|---|---|
| Matt. 11:12 | ". . . the kingdom of heaven suffers violence, and the violent *take it by force*." |
| John 6:15 | ". . . and *take* Him *by force* to make Him king." |
| Acts 23:10 | ". . . to *take* him [Paul] *by force* from among them." |
| Matt. 13:19 | ". . . the wicked one comes, and *snatches away* what was sown in his heart." |
| John 10:12 | ". . . and the wolf *catches* the sheep and scatters them." |
| John 10:28 | ". . . neither shall anyone *snatch* them out of My hand." |
| John 10:29 | ". . . and no one is able to *snatch* them out of My Father's hand." |
| Jude 23 | ". . . *pulling* [snatching] them out of the fire." |

| Acts 8:39 | "The Spirit of the Lord *caught away* Philip, . . ." |
| 2 Cor. 12:2 | "[The apostle Paul] was *caught up* to the third heaven." |
| 2 Cor. 12:4 | ". . . he [Paul] was *caught up* into paradise." |
| 1 Thess. 4:17 | ". . . shall be *caught up* together with them in the clouds to meet the Lord in the air." |
| Rev. 12:5 | ". . . her Child [Christ] was *caught up* to God." |

So the meaning and uniqueness of this particular Greek word, *harpazo,* is very clearly demonstrated. Philip was miraculously transported. Paul was caught up into heaven. And so also is this stated of Jesus Christ in Revelation 12:5.

Coupled together with the fact that this *harpazo*, or rapturing, includes the glorification and translation of LIVING saints (see also 1 Cor. 15:50–52) along with the resurrected dead saints of this age makes it all the more extraordinary, to say the least. And actually, it makes the subject all the more unique in anticipation. Just think of the moment when the whole collective "body of Christ" will be suddenly transported, "snatched," or "caught away" to meet Christ in the air, and taken to our residence in heaven! This is going to be a colossal event. All the rest of the world will be left behind. What will they think when they realize that all these people are suddenly missing?

Of course there are many other passages which expand on this theme of the Rapture of the Church, especially in Paul's epistles. This event involves all the members of the Church, from the Day of Pentecost until the "fullness of the Gentiles has come in" (Rom. 11:25). It involves both resurrected dead saints for the last 2000 years and the present living saints (1 Thess. 4:14–17). Everyone will be changed into new bodies and together will be caught away suddenly, as it were, "in the twinkling of an eye" (1 Cor. 15:51) and be transported up into heaven. This event was a "mystery" (1 Cor. 15:51 and Col. 1:27), meaning it was not known in past ages (Eph. 3:5). It is also referred to as the believer's "upward calling" (Philip. 3:14), and our "heavenly calling" (Col. 1:5 and 3:4). This was and still is the ever abiding "hope" of the Church of Jesus Christ (Col.

1:27). Obviously, this great event will bring to a close the present "Dispensation of Grace" (Eph. 3:2).

## *Beware of Hasty Comparisons!*

Please believe that it is easy to make superficial comparisons of certain words used in this passage from 1 Thessalonians concerning the Rapture with those descriptions of Christ's coming in judgment. I know because in my young Christian life I was deceived into doing it. The passage states that the Rapture will take place when Christ will "descend from heaven with a *shout,* with the voice of an *archangel,* and with the *trumpet* of God." One very subtle teacher planted in my mind the fact that at Christ's second coming to judge the earth, He is said to *"shout"* (Jer. 25:30, 31; Isa. 30:30; 42:13; Joel 2:11; Amos 1:2 and 2 Sam. 22:14). And it is also said that the *"archangel"* will be present at that time (Dan. 12:1, 2 and Rev. 19:17). In addition, at Christ's second coming there will be the *"trumpet* of God" sounded (Isa. 27:13; Zech. 9:14; Isa. 18:3 and Matt. 24:13). So I was led to quickly assume that Christ's coming for the Church must be the same coming described in these verses—and that will be at the close of the Great Tribulation!

However, this type of hasty comparison does not take into consideration the radical differences in the context of all these passages with that of 1 Thessalonians 4 and 1 Corinthians 15. Nowhere in all these previous passages does it mention the Rapture of the Church! There is not a solitary word in any of those passages to the effect of "catching away" both the resurrected dead and living saints of this Church age, and transporting them into heaven. In addition, in Paul's revelation in 1 Thessalonians 4, and in all the other passages speaking of the Rapture, Christ's mission is not the judgment and violent destruction on earth as is characterized by these other passages. Christ's mission is strictly to receive His body, the Church, like the bridegroom coming for his bride (Eph. 5:27). Consequently, it would be very hasty and superficial to automatically assume the two events are the same.

In fact, if there ever was a proof of the pretribulational Rapture of the Church, it would be found in the obvious *contrasts* between these two events. The "shout" of the Messiah for battle is certainly not the "shout" of Messiah for His bride. The contrast between the "trumpet" sound for war with the "trumpet" sound for the assembling of the saints is also obvious. In addition, the "archangel's" assistance for the nation of Israel must certainly be different than the "voice of the archangel" assisting in the collective gathering of the Church, wherein there is "neither Jew nor Gentile but one new man," to meet Christ in the air. You have two entirely different companies of people.

Actually, there are many trumpets spoken of in the Bible. God directed the movement of the nation of Israel by various and sundry trumpet sounds—see Numbers 10:1–10. One trumpet sound was for *assembling* the nation before God. A different trumpet sound was for *going to war*. In the case before us of the Rapture of the Church, there is the trumpet associated with the *gathering of the saints* to Christ. In contrast, at the second coming of Christ to judge the earth, there is the sound of the trumpet *for war*. Obviously, the two should never be confused. In a similar manner, there is the "shout" and the "roar" of Messiah for battle and for war at His second coming to earth as the references above speak. This should never be mixed with the "shout" of Christ for raising the dead (see John 5:28 and 11:43) and transforming the living at the Rapture. The shout of the bridegroom for the bride is most certainly not a shout for battle! And of course, there are different works the archangel will engage in. One is for the protection of Israel (Dan. 12:1) and another is due to the angelic interest in God's grace manifested in the Church (Eph. 3:10; Heb. 1:13, 14 and 1 Pet. 1:12). Let us always remember that the Devil uses the Bible, but he uses it wrongfully and only to bring confusion.

### *A Most Important Lesson*

At the time of Christ's first appearance, the people of Israel saw only *ONE* coming of the Messiah. They failed to distinguish between "the *sufferings* of Christ and the *glory* that was *to follow*" (1 Pet. 1:11). In fact, sometimes these two distinct comings of Messiah were found in the very same verses—see as examples Isaiah 61:1–4 with Luke 4:16–21; Isaiah 9:6–7; 11:1–6; Zechariah 9:9, 10, etc. It was a cardinal failure on the part of hardhearted, unbelieving Israel to accept this reality. This failure to distinguish between these two events brought Israel to confusion and eventual destruction. Only the Holy Spirit could enlighten the Jewish believer to differentiate between the two aspects of Messiah's work. This was a most important lesson.

Now however, the purpose of this Bible study is to demonstrate that precisely the same is true about the return of Christ at the conclusion of this age. It will actually be in *TWO* distinct phases. Because of the clear distinctions in the work which Christ is going to do, we must understand that the second coming of Jesus Christ is, as some have stated, in two distinct phases—the first, a "mystery" aspect for catching away the Church and terminating the present age, and the second, for the final judgment on rebellious nations in wrath and reigning in power on earth in and through Israel. Only the same Holy Spirit can open our eyes to see these important distinctions and truth. Actually, the coming of Christ for the Church is not His coming to the earth, but rather to meet Him in the air and be taken to heaven. This event was unknown in the Hebrew Scriptures. Whereas, the coming of Christ to the earth in cataclysmic judgment is the subject of many passages in the Hebrew Scriptures and the Gospels.

### *Carefully Examining Passages from Matthew which speak of Christ Coming to Reign on Earth*

Now let us just take the book of Matthew, which more surely focuses upon the future Kingdom of Christ. We will look at the passages which speak of the second coming of Christ at the end of the Great Tribulation to rule and reign on earth over God's people, and compare them with this theme of the Rapture of His Church. If the Rapture theme of Paul fits these passages, then we can all agree that the Rapture will be after the Great Tribulation. If, however, the Rapture is not to be found in these passages, then the Rapture obviously must occur at a different time—and the only time available would be earlier.

### First will be **Matthew 3:10–12**.

Note carefully, that in this passage, John the Baptist, who is preparing the way of the Lord, was speaking of the Lord's judgment on earth when He comes, and of His gathering those who bear good fruit into the prophesied Kingdom on earth—

> (10) And even now the ax is laid to the root of the **trees.** Therefore every tree which does not bear good fruit is cut down and thrown into the fire. (11) I indeed baptize you with water unto repentance, but He Who is coming after me is mightier than I, Whose sandals I am not worthy to carry. He will baptize you with the Holy Spirit and fire. (12) His winnowing fan is in His hand, and He will thoroughly clean out His threshing floor, and gather **His wheat** into the barn; but He will burn up **the chaff** with unquenchable fire.

Two metaphors are used by John the Baptist in this passage. In the first (v. 10), *"trees"* represent the people who will be on earth when the Messiah comes. The trees which do not bear good fruit are to be cut down and destroyed. These obviously represent the evil unbelievers. In contrast, the trees which have born good fruit are preserved for the Kingdom and represent the saints who go alive into the Kingdom Age. Similarly, in the second metaphor (v. 12), the ***grain field*** represents mankind. In this case, *"His wheat"* represents the saints who are collected to enter the Kingdom, whereas *"the chaff"* represents the lost who do not enter the Kingdom and will be destroyed.

In both cases, the individuals represented by the *fruitless trees* and the *chaff* are to be destroyed and taken out of this world. In both cases, those saints represented by the *fruitful trees* and the *wheat* remain and/or are gathered into the Kingdom. In other words, the saints who are alive and living for Christ immediately before He comes are simply preserved alive to enter into the Kingdom at Christ's coming, whereas the lost are to be destroyed and burned in the fire. *There is no stated Rapture of the saints!*

Between these two metaphors is a promised twofold baptism, which the Messiah will perform upon mankind at that future time. A part of mankind is said to be baptized by the Holy Spirit, whereas another part of them is understood to be baptized by fire.

In this context, the baptism of fire is their destruction and death as represented in verses 10 and 12. So the "fire" that is mentioned three times in this context is to be understood as the same in each case—a judgment from God upon the lost, unbelieving sinners. In addition, as most students of prophecy know and understand, there shall be a great outpouring of the Holy Spirit as prophesied in the Hebrew Scriptures, which takes place specifically at the beginning of Messiah's Kingdom reign on earth—see Psalm 104:30 with Isaiah 11:6–8; 32:15–18; 44:1–5; Ezekiel 11:17–20; 36:24–30; 39:25–29 and Joel 2:28, 29. This is the baptism of which John was speaking. This baptism represents God's special blessings upon the righteous who will live and enter into the Millennial Kingdom reign of Messiah on earth. Please remember that John the Baptist knew nothing of the Church of Jesus Christ that has existed for the last two thousand years. Though there are some similarities in terminology with the baptism of the Holy Spirit that began on Pentecost for this present age, they are most certainly not identical.

If we can position ourselves in John's place at this time, we can better appreciate what he is saying. John had been sent as the forerunner to the Messiah. He was expecting the Messiah to set up His Kingdom very soon. He was proclaiming to all the crowds of people before him that the promised Messiah was about to come and judge the earth. John was warning them that Messiah would segregate all the people into two camps. Those believers in the Messiah, prepared by repentance and righteous living, would be blessed and gathered into the Kingdom. In shocking contrast, those nonbelievers who remain non-repentant would be cast out and destroyed in a fiery judgment. Of course, John was not aware of the soon reality of Israel's national rejection of her King and of the consequent postponement of that Kingdom. He was also unaware of the intervening 2000 years of the present mystery Age of Grace. Therefore, these events predicted by John will actually be fulfilled after this Age of Grace has been concluded.

Consequently, we can summarize from this passage the three times it describes the righteous on earth who will enter into the Messiah's Kingdom. First, are the *good fruit trees* which are not cut down and burned in the fire. Second, are those blessed by the *baptism of the Holy Spirit* and not destroyed by the fire. And third, those who constitute the *wheat* will be gathered into the barns instead of being burned up in the fire. Now these represent the saints on earth who are not destroyed, but remain alive and are privileged to enter the Kingdom Age of Messiah.

We can naturally ask the question—Is the Rapture of the saints up into heaven as described by the apostle Paul in any of these cases? *Obviously, and in all honesty, it is not!* In the case of the Rapture of the Church, the saints are suddenly taken up and out of this earth at Christ's coming for them, whereas the lost are left alive on earth. In contrast, in each of these cases the saints are left alive on earth, whereas the wicked are taken to be destroyed. The Rapture of the saints is admittedly, by any honest person, not in view in this passage. In addition, this passage will set the stage for our understanding other similar passages in the book of Matthew about this same event which will take place at the second coming of the Messiah, Jesus Christ, to rule and reign.

Let us look at the next references and we shall see obvious similarities.

## Second, **Matthew 13:24–30 and 36–43**.

This is the famous parable of the wheat and the tares which Christ gave to indicate who it is who will enter the Kingdom age. I will paraphrase the parable and then quote in detail the interpretation as Christ gave it. A man planted good seed in his field, but an enemy came and planted tares in the field while the workers slept. When both kinds of plants grew up, it was determined that they should wait until the harvest to separate the tares from the wheat. Now let us read Christ's detailed explanation of the parable—

"He answered and said to them:
'He who sows the good seed is *the Son of Man*. The field is *the world*. The good seeds are *the sons of the Kingdom*, but the tares are *the sons of the wicked one*. The enemy who sowed them is *the Devil*. The harvest is *the end of the age*, and the reapers are *the angels*.

Therefore as the tares are gathered and burned in *the fire*, so shall it
    be *at the end of this age*.
The Son of man will send out His angels, and they will gather
    out of His Kingdom all things that offend, and those
    who practice lawlessness, and will cast them into *the
    furnace of fire*. There will be wailing and gnashing of
    teeth.
*Then the righteous* will shine forth as the sun in the Kingdom of
    their Father. He who has ears to hear let him hear.'

You can immediately see that this is similar to the account of
Matthew three. The Messiah is scheduled to one day reign on earth.
Prior to His reign there is going to be a planting and harvesting time
directly in preparation for that Kingdom here on this earth. It will
be much like the time of Christ's own ministry for some 3 ½ years.
The difference is that in the future this evangelism will cover the
whole world. (Interestingly enough, the book of Revelation tells us
of the worldwide service of the "144,000" for another period of 3
½ years—see Rev. 7 and 14.) The "end of the Age" in view is the
conclusion of this evangelism and the time of judgment just prior to
the Kingdom. The "good seed" represents the righteous who grow up
and mature in that growing season and will simply be gathered alive,
here on earth, and be privileged to enter into the future Kingdom of
Messiah. In contrast, the "tares" represent the unrighteous who will
not be allowed to enter into that Kingdom, but will be destroyed by
the fire of God's judgment.

Again, I ask the question, "*Is the Rapture,* as described by the
apostle Paul, in view in this parable?" *Obviously, and in all honesty,
the Rapture is not to be found here!* At the Rapture of the Church,
the saints will be suddenly caught up out of this world into heaven
and the unrighteous will be left alive and intact on earth. No one is to
be immediately destroyed. Actually, the ones left behind are those to
be tested in the Great Tribulation as represented in this parable. Here
in this parable, the field is the *world* over which the Messiah will
reign. In this case the righteous are simply preserved and gathered
into that Kingdom here *on earth*, whereas the wicked are destroyed.

By now you can also begin to reason that the Rapture of the Church would of necessity have had to take place at an earlier date—a date prior to this testing time. Obviously, the Rapture could not take place at some later date because the saints of the later time are all accounted for; they will come out of the Great Tribulation and enter alive into the Kingdom Age right here on earth.

### The Third is **Matthew 24:29–31, 36–41 and 45–51**.

This is the great chapter in Matthew wherein Christ explains the nature and events of the future Great Tribulation (24:21) time frame. As a special feature of this passage Christ is, in effect, telling the saints who live at that future time period what to look for and how to conduct themselves in preparation for the Messiah's coming. At least three times in this passage, Christ tells of saints who will be prepared to meet Him when He comes to reign on earth. Let us look at each one—

In <u>verses 29–31</u> Christ speaks of the miraculous regathering of the "elect." "*And he will send His angels with a great sound of a trumpet, and **they will gather together His elect from the four winds, from one end of heaven to the other** (verse 31).*" Some have mistakenly claimed that this has reference to the Rapture of the Church. However, it is instead a reference to the prophesied final regathering of the Jewish people. A close look at Deuteronomy 30:1–6 shows the original prophecy. It uses the same language and context. There Moses told of the same last days, wherein Israel, having been scattered throughout all the nations on the face of the earth, will be miraculously regathered—"*If any of you are driven out to the farthest parts under heaven, from there the LORD your God will gather you, and from there He will bring you. Then the LORD your God will bring you to the land which your fathers possessed, and you shall possess it.*" Nehemiah also quoted this same prophecy (Neh. 1:8, 9).

So, in this case, those gathered are the Jewish people. They are collected from "the farthest parts under heaven (that is, from all over the earth)." And they are collected back to "the land" of their original inheritance. *There is no Rapture here!*

In <u>verses 36–41</u> Christ speaks of those "taken" at that time of judgment. Notice that Christ compares it to the time of Noah's day—"*But as the days of Noah were, so also will the coming of the Son of Man be. For as in the days before the flood, they were eating and drinking, marrying and given in marriage, until the day that Noah entered the ark, and did not know until the flood came **and took them all away**, so also will the coming of the Son of Man be. Then two men will be in the field: one will be **taken** and the other left. Two women will be grinding at the mill: one will be **taken** and the other left.*" Again, some have confused this with the Rapture of the Church. However, the context is very clear and cannot be misunderstood—those taken are "taken" at this time in judgment just as those of Noah's day. As confirmation to this, the Gospel of Luke records that the apostles asked Christ "Where, Lord [will these people be taken]?" And the Lord answered, "Where the body is, there also will the vultures be gathered" (Luke 17:33–37). That makes it clear where they are to be taken—namely, in judgment. Thus it is, the ones left alive are the ones who will go into the blessed Kingdom age. *There is no Rapture here!*

In <u>verses 45–51</u> Christ spoke of the "servants" who will enter the millennial Kingdom—"*Who then is a faithful and wise servant, whom his master made ruler over his household, to give them their food in due season? Blessed is that servant whom his master, when he comes, will find so doing. Assuredly, I say to you that he will make him ruler over all his goods.*" Christ then stated concerning the wicked servant—"*. . . and appoint him his portion with the hypocrites. There shall be weeping and gnashing of teeth.*" The servants here are not raptured into heaven as described by the apostle Paul. Rather, they are simply allowed to go on doing service for the King in the Kingdom Age. The evil servants are destroyed. *In this whole section there is no Rapture!*

Actually, the parables of the Wise and Foolish Virgins (Matt. 25:1–13) and of the Talents (Matt. 25:14–30) are similar in nature and understanding to the parable of the faithful servant. We can make secondary spiritual applications from these parables to ourselves today. However, we must remember that they are not directly talking about the Church nor do they mention the Rapture of the Church.

They fit perfectly the saints of the future Tribulation period who will go into the Kingdom Age.

The fourth passage is **Matthew 25:31–46**.

Without quoting all this passage, everyone agrees that it speaks of the judgment of the "nations" which takes place at the second coming of the Messiah. The "sheep" and the "goats" are representative of the two classes of people who have been alive on earth prior to the Messiah's coming. The "sheep" represent the saved and the "goats" represent the unsaved. The "sheep" are those who served Christ during the Great Tribulation time period. They are rewarded with the words—*"Come, you blessed of My Father, inherit the Kingdom prepared for you from the foundation of the world"* (verse 34). The "goats" represent those who did not serve Christ during the same time period. To them it is stated—*"And these will go away into everlasting punishment"* (verse 46).

Once again, and in finality, *there is no Rapture in this passage*! This is consistent and similar to all the other passages in Matthew on this subject. The "sheep," representing Messiah's people who serve Him during the Tribulation testing time, simply go alive into the blessed Kingdom Age. They stay right here on earth. They are going to repopulate the earth in the Kingdom Age. They are not bodily glorified. They are not suddenly caught up into heaven. They are not taken out of this world. Their inheritance is the Kingdom, prophesied throughout the Hebrew Scriptures and specially prepared for them.

## *CONCLUSION !*

All these previously mentioned accounts bare striking similarity. Each of the accounts is complete by itself. In each account there are the saved and the unsaved living during a time of testing. In each account, at the coming of the Messiah, the saints remain alive and are allowed to inhabit the Kingdom reign here on earth. In each account the unsaved are judged and destroyed. None of the saints in any of these episodes are said to receive "glorified" bodies and, most importantly, none are said to be suddenly "caught up" to meet Christ in the air. Not only is the Rapture not found in any of these passages, but the Church itself is not found there, either. Very plainly then, the Rapture of the Church saints of this present Age of Grace does not take place at the end of the Great Tribulation time period at the second coming of Christ.

Since each of these passages tells us exactly who goes in, alive on earth, to occupy the Kingdom Age, it automatically means that the Rapture of the Church could not take place simultaneously with these events. It is impossible to split up these saints into two groups—one group caught up into heaven, while the other group goes into the Kingdom on earth. And this fact automatically means that the Rapture of the Church, as revealed through the apostle Paul, must have taken place at an earlier date just before the Great Tribulation time period. This is the only possible explanation and synchronization of these two distinct events. Therefore, one must distinguish between the mystery Rapture of the saints, which brings to a conclusion this Age of Grace, from that gathering of the saints of the Great Tribulation in order to begin the Kingdom Age.

In simplicity, and in a very abbreviated form, this is why I know that the Rapture of the Church of Jesus Christ is a separate and distinct event which terminates the end of the Age of Grace. It must be distinguished from that great and powerful event of the judgment on earth at the end of the Great Tribulation time period when Messiah comes to earth and chooses those saints still living to populate the Kingdom Age here on the earth.

My Christian friend, to whom I first gave this simple explanation and comparison, never challenged a single Scripture, or a single conclusion.

# THE RESTRAINING ONE

*A Bible Study on 2 Thess. 2:1–12*

## Notes by Jack W. Langford

First edition, Feb., 1997
Second edition, April, 2014

### *INTRODUCTION*

The apostle Paul was used by God in the conversion of a sizable number of residents in the Grecian city of Thessalonica. He not only taught them the basics of salvation and godly Christian living; he also taught them truths about the second coming of Jesus Christ and even about the appearance of the Antichrist, whom he designated as "the Man of Sin" and "the lawless one" (2 Thess. 2:3 and 8).

Paul was forced to leave Thessalonica because of persecution. A short time later he wrote the first epistle which spelled out in clear definition two aspects of these great end time events. First, there was the clear statement, regarding what has come to be called "the blessed hope" for the believers, which was new revelation—"this we say unto you by the Word of the Lord" (1 Thess. 4:15). They would experience not only the resurrection of saints who had fallen asleep in death, but the living saints as well would be changed and transported, together with the resurrected dead, up into the air to meet Christ at His coming for them (1 Thess. 4:13–18). Then, in the next chapter of the epistle, Paul spoke of the prophetic "Day of the Lord," involving Christ's coming in solemn judgment and wrath to be poured out upon the unbelievers (1 Thess. 5:1–11). This was not new revelation. It had been prophesied by the Hebrew prophets and by the Lord Jesus Christ during His earthly ministry to Israel (see Matt. 24 and 25). The order in which Paul revealed and explained these two events is, no doubt, the simple order in which they will occur. What we now popularly call "the Rapture of the Church" will take place first. The Rapture is in close proximity to, and will immediately be followed by "the Day of the Lord," which is primarily characterized by wrath.

A short time later Paul wrote his second inspired letter to the Thessalonians, bringing three areas of concern to their attention. The first concern had to do with the severe persecution the Thessalonians were suffering—chapter one. The second had to do with false teaching which had been propagated to the Thessalonians about the timing of events surrounding the Day of the Lord and the Rapture of the Church—chapter two. The third concern had to do with the laziness, or rather deliberate idleness, of certain members of the congregation—chapter three. In this present Bible study we are going to focus upon an aspect of chapter two concerning the One Who is said to be "restraining" the appearance of this "Man of Sin," also called "the Antichrist."

## A FALSE REPORT

It had apparently been propagated among the Thessalonians by false reports, as if from Paul himself, that the "Day of Christ (or the Lord) *had come*" (2 Thess. 2:2, NKJV). In other words, some had said that the time period of the "Day of the Lord" was already present in the world. In addition, these individuals were saying that Paul, himself, had taught this. Of course that teaching would soberly startle the saints into an immediate, false expectancy of all that was involved in the Day of the Lord. Perhaps some had even used this as an excuse to stop working. It would also cause confusion in their minds about when they would be caught up to meet Christ in the air, since Paul had mentioned that event first in his first epistle to them. Thus, this second Chapter of 2 Thessalonians was written to clear up misconceptions which were formed due to the false reports they had heard.

In verse one of chapter two Paul introduced the subject on the basis of the Lord's coming and the gathering of the saints together to the Lord—*"Now, brethren, concerning the coming of our Lord Jesus Christ and our gathering together to Him, . . ."* This was most certainly intended to be a comforting hope (1 Thess. 4:18). This hope, situated as it is at the beginning of Paul's discussion here, would also indicate that it was the first thing on the agenda for the future anticipation of the saints. It became, therefore, a double comfort for them in that it should not be erased by the thought of their plunging into the time of the "Great Tribulation," which characterizes the future "Day of the Lord."

## *"THE DAY OF THE LORD"*

The fact that the Thessalonians may have erroneously thought that they could actually already be living in the time of "the Day of the Lord" indicates that the expression, "the Day of the Lord," as it is used here, does not mean its narrow restricted sense of the actual second coming of Christ in judgment. The second coming of Christ in judgment upon the world is most often what is meant by the term, "the Day of the Lord." However, this expression is also sometimes used in its broader and all inclusive sense of meaning the whole time frame of events surrounding the second coming. This includes the events immediately preceding the second coming of the Messiah, His actual second coming, and then the Kingdom which would follow. This, of course, should be distinguished from "The day of Christ" as it relates to the Church. The expression, "the Day of Christ," is sometimes used synonymously with the truth of the Rapture of the Church.

The time frame of "the Day of the Lord" would include the seven year covenant of Antichrist wherein God will re-activate His specific dealings with the nation of Israel, resuming the sacrificial services in the Temple. The last 3 ½ years of this period is called "The Great Tribulation" (Matt. 24:15–31). This will be climaxed by the glorious and powerful event of Christ's second coming to execute judgment and to reign on earth. In Revelation 1:10 we actually have an illustration of this broader use. It can be literally translated that John "came to be in the Spirit on the Lord's Day, or the Day of the Lord." Thus John was inspired to write of all the events revealed to him about this seven year time period, including the Great Tribulation, the second coming of Christ in judgment and finally His Millennial Reign on earth. All this is the subject of the book of Revelation and comes under the heading, "The Day of the Lord."

## TWO INDICATORS

Paul then stated two very important qualifications which must exist before anyone could know that he was in the time frame of "the Day of the Lord." The "first" is what is most commonly translated in our Bibles as "the apostasy" (meaning a falling away or departure from the faith). The second is that "the Man of Sin" must make his appearance. Both these indicators must take place before anyone could know that he was in the "Day of the Lord." Since neither of these had taken place at the time Paul wrote to the Thessalonians, it is obvious that the Day of the Lord had not come as the false reports had stated. Concerning these two indicators, which must exist before the Day of the Lord would be present, information can be gathered from other parts of the Scriptures to fill in our understanding about them. We will now draw on that information.

### ONE,
### *"THE APOSTASY" or*
### *"The Departure"*

In the thinking of most, "the falling away" (King James Version) is more literally "the apostasy," or the defection from the faith. The Greek word used here is the noun *"apostasia"* and is only transliterated as "apostasy." On the other hand, the verb from which it is taken simply means "departure." Whenever the word is used in a *religious sense or context,* it is consistently translated as "apostasy," meaning a defection from God or the faith. This is true in the Greek version of the Hebrew Scriptures called the Septuagint

(Josh. 22:22; 2 Chron. 29:19; 39:19; Jer. 2:19 and 29:32, etc.). The same is true in the Greek Apocrypha (1 Macc. 6:14). Finally, in the Greek New Testament the word is understood the same way as used in a religious sense—Acts 21:21 is translated "to forsake [Moses]." Therefore, the Greek Lexicons will always give the first and primary definition of the word, *apostasia,* with the meaning of "defection or departure [from truth] in apostasy." In addition, the word is next of kin to *"apostasion,"* which means "divorcement" (Matt. 5:31; 19:7 and Mark 10:4). Therefore we can also say, by way of further clarification, that this religious apostasy will be a "divorcement" from the truths of Christ and true biblical Christianity.

However, it is also a fact that certain important lexicons, like the standard *Liddell and Scott Greek Lexicon* will also state a secondary meaning, when the word is not used in a religious sense, as simply— "departure or disappearance"—meaning only the physical departure or disappearance of a person or group from a position or place. For instance, I have *A Concordance of the Septuagint*, by George Morrish, who lists under *"apostasia,"* 1 Kings 20:13. There we are told of Jonathan's words to David, ". . . and thou shalt *depart* in peace, and the Lord shall be with thee, . . ." This, therefore, is an illustration of what is stated in *Liddell and Scott.* Consequently, several careful Bible teachers have taken a second look at this passage in 2 Thessalonians 2 in order to allow the context to make the determination of exactly what is meant. In other words, is Paul saying a religious "apostasy" must first come, or is he saying the "departure" of the Church must first come?

I must say, after a long delay, I have come to understand along with certian other Bible teachers, that the apostle Paul is herein saying the *"departure* of the Church must first come."

Briefly stated, the reasons for this are as follows:

(1) There is no indication in the context that this verse is discussing the "apostasy" of the Church. The apostasy of the Church is obviously a later revelation in Paul's later epistles (1 Tim. 4:1–5; 2 Tim. 3:1–17 and 4:1–5) and in the Jewish epistles (2 Pet. 2; 1 John 2:18–23; 4:1–6; 2 John 7–11 and Jude 5–19). All scholars agree that the book of 2 Thessalonians was one of the very first inspired letters written.

(2) In addition, "apostasy," as a defection from the faith, is not a singular event one could pinpoint, but rather a long standing condition which is hardly discernable as to just when it happened. Consequently, a religious defection before the appearance of Antichrist could only have reference to a long standing problem.

(3) Neither could this be the apostasy brought about by the "Man of Sin," himself. This *"apostasia"* Paul speaks of does not follow Antichrist's appearance, but rather precedes his appearance. Paul's words are clear that this *"apostasia"* comes *"first."*

(4) The context of this passage supplies us with two very important examples of a physical "departure"—that of the Church, itself! First, the very first verse states ". . . concerning the coming of our Lord Jesus Christ and *our gathering together to Him*, . . ." Second, others have pointed out that the immediate context also supplies us with an exact two-part parallel in similar language. Note the following—

| Verse 3 | Verses 7 and 8 |
|---|---|
| ". . . unless the | "He who now restrains will do so until He is |
| *departure comes first,* and *the Man of Sin* is revealed, . . ." | *taken out of the way.* And then *the lawless one* will be revealed." |

Consequently, after seeing these important facts, I had no choice but to embrace the position that verse 3 is, in fact, talking about the "departure" of the Church. In addition, the purpose of this study is to focus upon the identity of the "He" in verse 7. Just who is this "Restraining One"?

## TWO,
### *"THE MAN OF SIN"*

**The second indicator** that one would be in the midst of the "Day of the Lord" is the appearance of the "Man of Sin" or "Son of Perdition," whom we commonly call "the Antichrist." Paul speaks about him in verses 3–12 in this section of 2 Thessalonians 2. Christ spoke of him as recorded in the Gospel of Matthew, 24:15. In the book of Daniel we have the primary information about this coming world ruler under several different chapters and figures (see Dan. 7:8, 11, 20–26; 8:9–14, 23–26; 9:27; 11:21–45 and 12:11). This world ruler of the last days will be the head of a ten nation confederacy. He will become a very successful ruler causing "craft to prosper." He will bring about temporary peace and successfully put down any opposition through the use of mighty force at his disposal. He will be lifted up with such pride as will cause him to declare himself as "god" and suppress all other religions, including "warring against the saints" of God at that time. He will apparently engineer a seven year peace between Israel and other nations. In the middle of that time he will break the covenant, enter into Jerusalem and the Temple and defile it, making the Temple of God his own headquarters in blasphemy. The last 3 ½ years of his reign will be the time of "the Great Tribulation." Christ will destroy the Antichrist by the power and brightness of His coming. Remember also, that actually Paul had already told the saints at Thessalonica some things about this "Man of Sin" when he was present with them (2 Thess. 2:5). Now Paul is telling them that there was One preventing or "restraining" the appearance of the Antichrist.

## "THE RESTRAINING ONE"

At this juncture, the apostle Paul introduced another factor or Person, the One Who "restrains" the appearance of the Antichrist and his program of lawlessness. The identity of the One restraining has been hotly debated for many years, partly because there seems to be a bit of mystery as to His identity. Paul did not actually name the Restrainer or spell out specifically what it is, if it is not a person. I will show in this study that the identity of the Restrainer becomes obvious in light of biblical truths. Many people simply don't want to accept the clear implications against their own theories if the identity is, in fact, the Person of the Holy Spirit.

In this regard, it should be noted at the beginning, that whoever this Restrainer is, this was no mystery to the Thessalonians. It was common knowledge to them, as Paul indicated—"And now you know *what* is restraining, . . . *He Who* now restrains . . . ." (verses 6 and 7). This strongly implies that every reader of this letter, which Paul encouraged to be read everywhere (see 1 Thess. 5:27), should also know this "Restrainer." And if every believer should know Him, certainly we should know Him! As we compare Scripture with Scripture, there will be confirmed to us the simple and common knowledge as to Who this Restrainer is—

## THE RESTRAINER IS THE HOLY SPIRIT

### The Scriptural Reasons Are:

**No. 1) The Holy Spirit of God has always been a restraining force against evil.**
The Scriptures will testify of this for different Ages:

When the world came to be in rebellion against God in the days of Noah, God said, *"My Spirit will not always strive with men, . . ."* (Gen. 6:3). In other words, the restraint of the Spirit of God against wickedness would cease in that age, and then the judgment would come. This is similar to what will happen at the end of this Age.

On behalf of the nation of Israel, when they were in obedience to God's Word, God would often protect them through the agency of the Holy Spirit restraining the enemy. *"When the enemy shall come in like a flood, the Spirit of the Lord shall lift up a standard against him"* (Isaiah 59:19).

In addition, when Israel herself rebelled against God, it was said, *"But they rebelled, and vexed His Holy Spirit"* (Isaiah 63:10).

Also, for and during this present Church Age, it is stated, "And when He has come (the Holy Spirit), He will convict the world of sin, and of righteousness, and of judgment: . . ." (John 16:8). That means that the Holy Spirit is a restraining influence during this Age. Thus, in every age the Holy Spirit has been a restraining factor against sin and rebellion. Consequently, we can see why this was no mystery. This was common knowledge to both Jewish and Gentile believers in the Church.

## No. 2) The Holy Spirit is specifically said to be a restraining factor against the spirit of Antichrist—1 John 4:2–4,

*By this you know the Spirit of God: Every spirit that confesses that Jesus Christ has come in the flesh is of God, and every spirit that does not confess that Jesus Christ has come in the flesh is not of God. And this is the spirit of the **Antichrist**, which you have heard **was coming**, and **is now already in the world**. You are of God, little children, and have overcome them, because **He Who is in you is greater** than he who is in the world.*

This Scripture is unmistakably similar to what the apostle Paul said in 2 Thessalonians 2. Paul said, "The mystery of lawlessness is already at work." John said the spirit of Antichrist is "now already in the world." Paul said the lawless one will yet be "revealed in his own time" at the future last day. John said the same, "You have heard [Antichrist] was coming," meaning in the future last day. Paul then indicated that there is a greater One Who is presently a "restraining" influence against the lawless one. John also said that the Holy Spirit in the believer "is greater" (more powerful) than the spirit of Antichrist, and thus is the One Who is containing or restricting his activity. Language could hardly be any plainer in giving us the identification of the One of Whom the apostle Paul was speaking.

## No. 3) The Administration of the Holy Spirit is in opposition to the Administration of Lawlessness under Antichrist.

The Antichrist will eventually head the Administration of Lawlessness (2 Thess. 2:7, 8). Paul said this lawlessness is already "at work." Paul calls it "the mystery of lawlessness" (verse 7).

The present Church Age is operating under the direction of the Holy Spirit Who is now in residence on earth in the body of believers and is said to be operating the "Ministration [or Administration] of Righteousness" (2 Cor. 3:9, literal translation). Furthermore, this righteousness is referred to as "great is the mystery of Godliness" (1 Tim. 3:16). Obviously a corollary emerges. The Church and its

Ministration under the direction of the Holy Spirit is in opposition to "the Ministration of Lawlessness." The full unleashing of *lawlessness* without restrictions cannot go into effect until the impediment by the *Ministration of Righteousness* ceases. You can have some lawlessness during *"the reign of righteousness"* (Rom. 5:21), and you can have some righteousness during *"the reign of lawlessness"* (as in the Great Tribulation). However, you cannot simultaneously have *"the reign of lawlessness"* during *"the reign of righteousness"* because two contradictory and conflicting administrations cannot be in full operation at the same time. One must yield to the other.

It becomes obvious, therefore, that the present Administration of the Holy Spirit stands as a restraining force against the full unleashing of lawlessness headed by the Antichrist. The Holy Spirit of God, Who has taken up His residence on the earth since the beginning of the Church Age, must remove Himself "out of the midst" (2 Thess. 2:7, literal translation) of this earthly system so that Antichrist can reign. As long as the Holy Spirit is in residence upon the earth, Satan cannot take up his residence here in the person of Antichrist. As long as this "Ministration of the Spirit" continues, the reign of Antichrist will be held in abeyance. When the Holy Spirit does remove Himself "out of the midst," then the Antichrist will be revealed and will reign, being indwelt by Satan, himself.

This is somewhat similar in nature to what happened in Noah's day. Lawlessness kept pressing in upon the world. The Holy Spirit kept striving with mankind in restraint. But, "My Spirit will not always strive with men," God warned (Genesis 6:3). And when the time came for the Holy Spirit to cease striving, the horrible judgment of the flood came upon that ungodly world.

## No. 4) The amazing gender switch.

The One restraining in verse 6 is spoken of in the neuter gender, *"what (or that) is restraining,"* whereas, in verse 7 the same is spoken of in the masculine gender, *"He Who now restrains"* and *"He is taken out of the way."* This gender switch is one of the fingerprints to the identity of the Holy Spirit. The word "Spirit" in the Greek language is in the neuter gender, and yet the Spirit is a Person, and is spoken of in the masculine gender, *"He."* In Romans 8:16 and 26 we have the same phenomenon of the Holy Spirit being spoken of in the neuter gender, *"the Spirit Itself."* Though often translated "Himself," the word Spirit is literally neuter in gender. Yet throughout Romans chapter 8, the Holy Spirit is spoken of as a Divine Person Who indwells and intercedes on behalf of the believer. Thus, elsewhere the Holy Spirit is repeatedly referred to in the masculine gender, *"He."* See also such passages as John 14:26; 15:26 and 16:7–15 as examples.

## No. 5) Only a Divine Person can restrain this power of Satan.

If we remember that the rebellion of Antichrist is no ordinary rebellion and that it has been accumulating in potential for nearly 2000 years, then we can see that only the Holy Spirit of God could restrain it. In other words, the Restraining One was working in Paul's day, and is still doing so to the very end of this Age. In addition, Satan himself, personally on earth, will finally be energizing the Antichrist. Legions of fallen angelic beings will be assisting. Demons from Hell will be unleashed. The nations of earth will be in support of Antichrist. There simply are no human instruments, powerful individuals, governments, or angels who could be restraining all this. Only Divinity has the power.

## No. 6) No other satisfactory explanation.

It is properly said that there is absolutely no other restraining one, in common knowledge to believers, which can possibly or suitably fit the demands and magnitude of the requirement of this work as revealed in the Scriptures. Some have postulated that human government could be the restrainer because it was originally ordained of God to restrain evil among the nations. However, in the case of Antichrist, he and his system *will be the government*, and most certainly he will not be restraining himself. Some have suggested that Michael the archangel will be the restrainer. However, Michael's primary function will be to protect Israel during Antichrist's reign (Dan. 12:1), not to restrain Antichrist from appearing and functioning.

## No. 7) The removal of the Holy Spirit automatically causes the Rapture of the Church of Jesus Christ.

### *CONCLUDING REMARKS and DEDUCTION*
#### *The Holy Spirit and the Church Leave Together!*

We can understand that when the Holy Spirit of God removes Himself "from the midst" OF THIS EARTH, the Church of Jesus Christ, which is bound up "in the Spirit," will go with Him— Romans 8:11.

> *But if the Spirit of Him Who raised up Jesus Christ from the dead dwells in you, He Who raised up Christ from the dead will also give life to your mortal bodies through His Spirit Who dwells in you.*

Obviously, when the collective body of Christ, which was "baptized by One Spirit into one body" (1 Cor. 12:13), ascends into heaven (1 Cor. 15:51–54), the Holy Spirit, Who uniquely composes and indwells that body, will simultaneously ascend in them and they in Him. In fact, the Church's resurrection and Rapture will be by the power and agency of the Holy Spirit.

### *REMEMBER THE BIRTH OF THE CHURCH*

Let us look at this from the perspective of the birthday of the Church of Jesus Christ. Christ promised the Twelve that He would send the Holy Spirit to indwell them and to keep them (John 15,16 and 17). At the precise moment the Holy Spirit of God left heaven and took up His residence on earth in the lives of believers, collectively baptizing them into one body on the day of Pentecost some 2000 years ago, the Church of Jesus Christ was instantly created. One moment there had been just a group of believers praying; the next moment the Church of Jesus Christ was brought suddenly into existence. So it will be in a somewhat similar manner at the end of the Age. When the Holy Spirit suddenly removes Himself from this earth, the Church, as well, will no longer be present. One moment it will be there; the next instant it will be gone—G-O-N-E! The earth will no longer be the Holy Spirit's residence, and the earth will no longer be the Church's residence. The Church will be missing, the heavens being our destiny.

We can understand, therefore, since the Antichrist, at the head of a ten nation confederacy, will begin his "seven year covenant of peace" involving the nation of Israel and others, that the removing of the Holy Spirit and the Rapture of the Church is an absolute necessity immediately prior to that time period.

**Jack W. Langford**
**P.O. Box 801, Joshua, TX 76058**
**817-295-6454**
**www.SeparationTruth.com**
**langfordjw@sbcglobal.net**

CPSIA information can be obtained
at www.ICGtesting.com
Printed in the USA
FFOW05n1845290517

9 781498 404389